Religion and Life

with Christianity

Unit B

Ina Taylor

www.heinemann.co.uk
✓ Free online support
✓ Useful weblinks
✓ 24 hour online ordering

01865 888058

Heinemann
Inspiring generations

Heinemann Educational Publishers

Halley Court, Jordan Hill, Oxford OX2 8EJ

Part of Harcourt Education

Heinemann is the registered trademark of
Harcourt Education Limited

© Ina Taylor, 2005

First published 2005

09 08 07 06 05
10 9 8 7 6 5 4 3 2

British Library Cataloguing in Publication Data is
available from the British Library on request.

10-digit ISBN: 0 435302 28 0
13-digit ISBN: 978 0 435302 28 3

Designed and typeset by Artistix

Original illustrations © Harcourt Education Limited,
2005

Illustrated by Andrew Skilleter

Printed in Italy by Printer Trento srl

Cover photo © Getty Images/Photographer's Choice

Picture research by Elaine Willis

Acknowledgements

Every effort has been made to contact copyright holders
of material reproduced in this book. Any omissions will
be rectified in subsequent printings if notice is given to
the publishers.

The author and publisher would like to thank the
following for the use of copyright material:

Photographs – pp. 5, 8, 9, 23, 24, 33, 35, 69 (top left), 72,
78, 97, 100, 102, 104, 106 Corbis; pp. 6 (both), 7, 30, 54,
68 (both), 69 (bottom right) Getty Images/PhotoDisc;
p. 10 Harcourt Education/Tudor Photography; pp. 13, 59
Ina Taylor; p. 15 SPL; p. 17 Reuters; p. 19 Topfoto; p. 26
Art Archive; p. 29 Scala, Florence; pp. 36, 41 (right), 48,
52 Getty; pp. 41 (left), 64, 113 Alamy; pp. 44, 80 Rex;
p. 46 St Albans Observer; p. 50 Rex Features/Image
Source; p. 55 The Children's Society; p. 60 Equal
Opportunities Commission; p. 62 National Gallery;
p. 67 PA; p. 69 (top right) Getty Images/Digital Vision;
p. 70 The Church of England, Diocese of Birmingham;
p. 73 AP; pp. 77, 82, 87 BBC; p. 85 BBC Manchester;
p. 88 BBC/Roger Scruton; p. 90 BBC/Rhian AP Gruffyd;
p. 92 Kobal; p. 94 ITV/Granada; p. 111 MHA; p. 112 The
Salvation Army; p. 114 Still Pictures/Hartmut
Scwartzbach.

Realia – p. 16 NSPCC leaflet © NSPCC, photograph
posed by models © Matt Harris, p. 61 graph © the Office
for National Statistics website; p. 66 table and pie chart
© the Office for National Statistics website; p. 80 'It's
Madge-ic' © *The Sun*, 20 September 2004; p. 84 TV Guide
© PA News Ltd, pp. 101, 106 Cafod quotes © Cafod;
p. 106 ABCD logo © ABCD; p. 107 CBM leaflet © CBM;
p. 108 Christian Aid logo © Christian Aid; p. 109
Christian Aid case study © Christian Aid; p. 110 CHT
website reproduced by permission of Design Lynx Limited
and CHT © CHT (www.churchhousingtrust.org.uk);
pp. 112, 113 Salvation Army case studies © The
Salvation Army.

Exam questions – Exam questions have been reproduced
with the permission of Edexcel Limited. Edexcel Limited
accepts no responsibility whatsoever for the accuracy or
method of working in the answers given.

CONTENTS

HOW TO USE THIS BOOK

This book has been specifically written to prepare students for the Edexcel GCSE Religious Studies paper Unit B Religion and Life, which is based on the study of Christianity. The Edexcel exam has a two-hour paper for students who are answering the extended writing options, either Question 9 'Religion and the Media' or Question 10 'Religion: Wealth and Poverty'. These two topics receive extra coverage in the book to help students prepare those questions adequately. For even more material and activities on all six sections please refer to *Revise for Religious Studies GCSE Edexcel Specification A: Religion and Life* (Heinemann, 2004).

Coursework

Students who choose one of the coursework options sit a one-and-a-half hour exam paper. The two chapters on 'Religion and the Media' and 'Religion: Wealth and Poverty' can be used by students to assist them with their coursework preparation. There are ideas for personal research with links to websites for up-to-date information, as well as useful addresses to write to for information. The section dedicated to preparing, researching and writing coursework is designed to help students to achieve their best coursework grade.

Exam focus

Every double-page spread has activities designed to help students to develop their analytical and evaluative skills. The activities at the end of each chapter take this a stage further, with specific exam practice. There is one complete section of the book devoted to examples of exam questions for students to practise and helpful advice on how to approach certain types of questions. Using worked examples, students are encouraged to learn how the marking process operates so they can see how marks can be gained or lost. They are given the chance to 'be the examiner' with examples of varying levels to grade and comment on.

How the book is organised

For ease of use, the textbook follows the Unit B specification, beginning with the philosophical study 'Believing in God'. The book continues to follow the order of the exam paper with the extended writing options coming after the main units of study. Students preparing these topics as coursework, however, will probably start work on one of these areas ahead of many of the others.

The title page for each chapter tells a student what the exam paper expects them to know and lists the key terms for the chapter. These key terms with their meanings also reappear throughout the chapter to reinforce learning. The activity that appears on the chapter title page offers a useful introduction to the topic. Each double-page spread is designed to provide the material for a one-hour lesson, with activities to develop a student's thinking skills and build towards exam answers.

On some spreads under the heading 'Path to the top', students are offered extension information which they might like to use in the exam. Using this information will show the examiner that they have a broad understanding of the subject which may help to boost their grade.

At the end of each chapter 'Putting it all together' provides questions to help the student gain an overview of the topic.

Throughout the book the Bible is used as the source of authority for Christians and the *Good News Bible* has been used as the source for quotations.

1 BELIEVING IN GOD

In this chapter you will learn:

- how religious upbringing in a Christian family or community can lead to, or support, belief in God
- about the nature of religious experience for Christians as seen in numinous, conversion, miracles and prayer
- how these religious experiences may lead to, or support, belief in God
- how the appearance of the world (design and causation) may lead to, or support, belief in God
- how the search for meaning and purpose in life may lead to, or support, belief in God
- how the presence of religion in the world may lead to, or support, belief in God
- how non-religious explanations of the world and of miracles may lead to, or support, agnosticism or atheism
- how unanswered prayers and the existence of evil and suffering (including moral evil and natural evil) may lead people to question or reject belief in God
- why the existence of evil and suffering raises problems for people who believe in God as omnipotent, benevolent and omniscient
- how Christians respond to this problem.

Figure A *The night sky. What does this image make you think about?*

The key terms you must know the meaning of are:

numinous, conversion, miracle, prayer, design argument, causation argument, agnosticism, atheism, moral evil, natural evil, omnipotent, benevolent, omniscient

ACTIVITY

1. Look at Figure A. List some thoughts people might have about the existence, or not, of God if they stared into a night sky. Make a brief note against each point to say why they might think that.

1 What is the point of it all?

AIM

To understand why some people believe in God, why others do not and why some people are unsure.

KEY TERMS

agnosticism not being sure whether God exists
atheism believing that God does not exist
prayer an attempt to contact God, usually through words

I believe there is a God. There are so many people in the world who believe in the existence of God. Okay, there are lots of different religions, but they accept that there is a higher power than us. There is no way they have all got it wrong. In fact there are great similarities in what they all believe even if they live in opposite parts of the globe and have never met. Besides, a lot of people have actually succeeded in communicating with God – **prayer**, that sort of thing – and it has often made a real difference to their lives. Of course God exists. The world didn't happen by accident, did it? The odds on that are far worse than winning the lottery!

Science is marvellous; I'd be the first to agree with that, but science doesn't disprove the existence of God. I think God works through science to help humans. Modern medicine is a perfect example. Can I just say that science will never be able to supply all the answers to everything. For example, there are always cases of people who recover from terrible illnesses that doctors say are untreatable. How do you answer that one? Miracles do happen!

Jessica believes in God.

What is the point of being on earth?

I do not believe in God. I'm an atheist. There's no evidence to convince me that God exists. Science is the way forward. Okay, maybe we don't know everything yet, but new discoveries are being made all the time. Eventually science will answer all our questions.

Miracles? They are just illusions, coincidences. You don't hear people boasting about all the prayers they have made that haven't been answered, do you? Then there are all the terrible disasters that happen where innocent people suffer, now I would say that definitely proves God doesn't exist.

People have made up the idea of a God because they are scared. They don't like the thought that there is nothing out there. It's always comforting to have somebody to turn to when things go wrong, isn't it? It's a bit like being a child really – expecting Mummy to pick you up when you fall over, or cuddle you when you have a bad dream. Grow up! There is nothing there. You've just got to get on with life. What's the point? Well, dare I say it, there isn't one!

Tanvi is an atheist.

I'm not sure whether God exists or not. I'm an agnostic. I'd like to see more proof to be sure there is a God. You say, what about science? Well yes, it's good at explaining how things work. I mean scientists have discovered all sorts of amazing facts about the universe. But let's face it, scientists didn't invent those things, they were already out there. Now surely something must have created them.

I want to know why we are here in the first place. The reason I'm not prepared to come down firmly on one side of the fence or the other is because I know we are only human. How can our brain understand something that is so much more advanced than us? I have trouble getting my head round the idea of what might have existed before the Big Bang!

Ed is an agnostic.

Does good always win over evil?

What happens when I die?

Why do people suffer when they haven't done anything wrong?

ACTIVITIES

Believer	Agnostic	Atheist

1. Draw a table like the one above, with the headings 'Believer', 'Agnostic', and 'Atheist'. Put the arguments each person on this spread gives for their views in the correct list. As a class, think of other points these three people could have given to add strength to their case.

2. In pairs, choose two of the people and role-play a discussion between them. Remember each is keen to convince the other one that they are right!

3. With a partner, decide what answers a **believer** and an atheist would give to the boxed questions on this spread.

4. Answer these questions.

a) What is meant by the word 'atheist'?

b) Outline the reasons a person might give for being agnostic.

For discussion

'God must exist because so many people believe.' Would you agree with this statement? Is it possible that such a large number of people have got it wrong?

1 Upbringing in a Christian family

AIM

To understand why an upbringing in a Christian family might lead some people to believe, or support their belief, in God.

KEY TERMS

benevolent the belief that God is good or kind
omnipotent the belief that God is all-powerful
omniscient the belief that God knows everything that has happened and everything that is going to happen

STARTER

Discuss with a partner what you think the teenagers in Figure B might gain from being brought up in a Christian family. Are there any difficulties it might cause for them?

In the family

A child born into a Christian family is likely to have the advantage of relatives and friends who can teach him or her about the Christian way of life.

Figure B *A Christian family at home. What do you think the advantages of being raised in a Christian family might be?*

First and foremost, children learn about Christianity from their parents but they are also likely to have godparents who will help them understand how to lead a Christian life. Godparents are people who have been specially chosen to help the child from infancy. A child is usually given godparents when they are baptised (see pages 10–11). Being surrounded by Christian believers gives a child the opportunity to ask about matters of faith he or she does not understand. Parents also try to set their children a good example of how to lead a Christian life.

Worship

Worship in the home is likely to be one of the things a child learns from his or her parents. How much worship takes place will depend on how observant the family are. A child is likely to be taught how to pray and the importance of prayer for Christians. It is likely that the child will learn how to recite the Lord's Prayer, the most important prayer Jesus taught his followers. The family may hold a daily act of worship that the child will be encouraged to join. This might take the form of a short grace before meals to thank God for providing food, or a prayer at bedtime asking God to keep the family safe through the night.

Festivals

Families usually celebrate the major Christian festivals of Easter and Christmas in the home. Children are taught about the meaning and the importance of these festivals.

Christmas

● A Christian family usually prepares for Christmas during Advent when children might be encouraged to light an Advent candle as they count the Sundays till Christmas.

Figure C A Christian family is likely to have a model nativity set as part of its Christmas decorations. Children in the family learn stories of Jesus' birth as they assemble it each year. In what other ways could parents help their children learn about Christianity?

- The family may read some of the Gospel stories associated with the festival and learn special carols that are sung at this time.
- Within the family children learn that Christmas is a time of giving. They are encouraged to donate to charity at this time as well as give presents to their friends and relatives.

Easter

- The Christian preparation for Easter may involve children joining their families in giving up a favourite food during Lent as they learn about Jesus' suffering.
- Receiving chocolate Easter eggs on Easter Sunday has a special meaning for children in a Christian family because they are aware of the symbolism of Jesus' resurrection from the tomb.

Why might a Christian upbringing support a person's belief in God?

Being born into a Christian family is likely to support someone's belief in God because they are surrounded by others who are convinced of the existence of God. If the religion has been handed down in a family, it might seem perfectly natural to children growing up in that family to believe in God.

Basic Christian beliefs about God a child might be taught in the home

- Christians believe there is only one God who wishes good for everyone (**benevolent**).
- Christians believe God is more powerful than anything else (**omnipotent**).
- Christians believe God has great knowledge and knows everything that happened in the past, what is going on at the moment, and what will happen in the future (**omniscient**). They believe that humans still have the freedom to behave as they choose. God may know what we are going to do, but God does not control our actions. We are not puppets.

ACTIVITIES

1. Make a list of the different ways a child might be encouraged to believe in God if he or she has been brought up in a Christian family. Look over your list, then rearrange it in order of importance.

2. Cut out six slips of paper. Write the words 'omniscient', 'omnipotent' and 'benevolent' on three of the slips. On the other three slips copy down the meaning of each word. Shuffle the papers up, then try to match the correct word to its meaning. Do it several times because it is a painless way of learning the meanings!

⬯ For discussion

Do you think children should be allowed to make up their own minds about whether or not to believe in God?

AIM

To understand why an upbringing in a Christian community might lead some people to believe, or support their belief, in God.

STARTER

Discuss with a partner why you think the teenagers in Figure D have chosen to go to church. What two questions would you like to ask them?

Baptism

Someone born into a Christian family is likely to be taken to church from an early age. The first occasion may well be as a baby of a few months old to be baptised. Some Christians choose to hold a baptism ceremony for infants to thank God for the child's safe arrival and to welcome them into the religion. Godparents are chosen for the child who promise before God that they will take a special interest in the child and help to bring them up as a Christian.

Some groups of Christians hold services of dedication for infants, preferring to wait until the person is old enough to make up their own mind about being baptised as a Christian.

The Baptist church holds believers' baptisms for young people and adults who have attended classes to learn about Christianity and who have asked to be baptised.

Worship

Most Christians will try to worship with their Christian community at a church or chapel. Worshipping with a group of believers can often strengthen a person's faith. Families bring their children to church for special family services which some churches hold once a month. This enables a family to worship together. These special services are adapted to suit younger members of the Christian community and no one minds too much if toddlers leave their seats to investigate other parts of the church!

Figure D *Why do you think worship plays an important role in a Christian family? Should children be free to refuse to join their parents in church? Why?*

Many Christian communities run a Sunday School where children go to learn about their religion in small classes. Sunday School often takes place at the same time as the main church service, enabling the parents to attend worship while their children are learning. The Sunday School might well prepare a nativity play at Christmas in order to teach the children the Gospel stories and give a performance to other members of the congregation.

Confirmation

People who were baptised as infants may want to make their own personal commitment to the Christian faith and confirm the promises made on their behalf when they were babies. A young Roman Catholic will often begin their personal commitment to Christianity by taking Holy Communion from the age of seven. A few years later, they may choose to become confirmed.

In the Anglican Church it is more usual for people to be in their teens or older when they are confirmed by the bishop. This is because the church wants to be sure a person is mature enough to make the important commitment to follow the Christian way of life. To prepare for their **confirmation**, they will attend classes with the priest to understand fully what the Christian way of life involves.

Being able to receive the sacrament of Holy Communion is one of the most important milestones in the religious upbringing of Anglicans and Catholics.

FOR RESEARCH

Find out more about confirmation. Why do you think someone brought up as a Christian might want to be confirmed? How might this strengthen their belief in God?

Being part of the church community

- As members of the Christian community, children may choose to become involved in activities organised by the church. This could take the form of joining a Christian youth club or other groups run along Christian lines such as Girls' or Boys' Brigade, Scouts, Guides or similar groups for younger children.
- At Christmas, younger members of the church may be invited to join with others to go carol singing.
- At Harvest Festival young people might become involved in the distribution of hampers of produce to the needy.

Through taking part in activities like these, children come to understand how Christians care for others and the different ways of putting the Christian message into practice. Some children may also find their beliefs strengthened if they attend a Church school. Although the curriculum will be the same as in other schools, there is likely to be a greater emphasis on learning and understanding the Christian way of life and putting it into practice.

ACTIVITIES

1. Based on what you have learned about a Christian upbringing, what answers do you think the teenagers in Figure D would give to your questions at the start of this spread?

2. Draw a table with two columns: 'Features of a Christian upbringing' and 'Effects of a Christian upbringing'. Use the information on these pages and on pages 8 and 9 (along with any other points you can think of) to fill in the column 'Features of a Christian upbringing'. Against each of your points, write the likely effect in the right-hand column. Which do you think is likely to be the most influential in supporting a Christian's belief in God? Could any of the points have the opposite effect? If so, why?

1 It's personal!

To understand why some religious experiences might lead to, or support, a Christian's faith in God and to understand a non-religious response to these phenomena.

KEY TERMS

conversion when your life is changed by giving yourself to God

miracle something which seems to break a law of science and makes you think only God could have done it

numinous the feeling of the presence of something greater than you, e.g. in a church or looking up at the stars

prayer an attempt to contact God, usually through words

The 'wow' factor!

Some people arrive at a belief in God without the assistance of their family or friends. Something happens to them that takes them by surprise and convinces them that there is a God. For some it might be the 'wow!' factor; they see something which completely takes their breath away and gives them a feeling of awe and wonder. This convinces them that they are in the presence of a greater power. The feeling is called the **numinous**. Some people experience it when they enter a religious building; for others it comes from a marvel of nature – a glorious sunset, the intricacy of a snowflake seen through a microscope or being present when a new life enters the world.

For some people this experience is so powerful it convinces them that God exists. There are others who are so profoundly moved by the experience that their life is never the same again. They undergo a religious **conversion**, which means they commit themselves to Christianity and strive to serve God by following the teachings of Jesus closely.

Prayer

Prayer is the most important and personal way for a Christian to communicate with God. Prayers may vary from giving thanks, to praising God or asking God for help. On occasions people believe their prayers are answered; maybe the sick person they asked God to heal does get better or the problem they asked for God's guidance on is solved. If a prayer is answered, that person's belief in God is strengthened.

When a prayer is not answered as a Christian hoped, then his or her faith can be challenged. It might lead him or her to wonder whether God exists or not, and become an agnostic. An unanswered prayer might convince others that God does not exist and lead them to become atheists. Christians would argue that God does listen to everyone's prayers and responds in the way God sees fit. Humans cannot possibly understand the mind of God.

For discussion

How do you think a believer would feel if they were not healed even though they had prayed to God?

PATH TO THE TOP

A useful term you might use is **mystical experience**, which means hearing God's voice or seeing a vision of a religious figure. Look up Acts 9: 1–31. What mystical experience convinced Saul to believe in God and become the apostle St. Paul?

ACTIVITY

1. Make a list of ten experiences which you think might lead some people to believe there is a God. Are there any that would convince you? Why?

Miracles

Miracles often cause controversy because they are **paranormal** happenings which break the natural laws of science. There are well-documented cases of people

Figure E *Some people's belief in God is triggered by the natural world. The feeling of awe and wonder they experience, which is called the numinous, convinces them that there is a greater power at work in the world. They believe that power is God. What other explanation is possible?*

praying to God for help and then, for example, recovering from an illness which medical science had said was incurable. There can be other miraculous happenings when, against all the odds, someone survives a natural disaster. For example, there have been instances of people, even babies, being rescued from the debris of a collapsed building several days after it had been destroyed by an earthquake.

Christians believe God can perform miracles. They point to evidence of miracles in both the Old Testament and the New Testament and to the fact that Jesus himself performed many miracles of healing as well as miracles over nature. For Christians, Jesus' resurrection from the dead is the greatest miracle of all.

People who have witnessed miracles are usually convinced they are seeing the work of God, and this strengthens their faith. Some argue that God uses miracles as a way of helping Christians to believe in him.

Miracles at Lourdes

In 1858, a young girl named Bernadette Soubrious had visions of the Virgin Mary at a cave near Lourdes in France. These visions have led many people to visit the cave to pray and drink water from the nearby spring, hoping God will perform a

miracle and heal them. So great is their faith that 6645 Christians claim to have been healed as a result of their visit to Lourdes. Claims of miraculous healing are fully investigated by a committee of doctors before they are accepted as miracles and only 66 have ever been officially accepted as miracles. The most recently confirmed miracle occurred in 1999 when Jean-Pierre Bely recovered from multiple sclerosis. Doctors said his cure was medically inexplicable and many called it 'a gift from God'.

On average, six million Christians make the pilgrimage to Lourdes every year, very few of whom will be healed of their illnesses. Most of these pilgrims, however, believe they receive a spiritual healing which strengthens their faith and gives them the power to carry on despite their difficulties.

ACTIVITIES

2. Draw a table with two columns. In one list the reasons why some people do not believe in miracles and in the other column list the reasons why some Christians believe in miracles.

3. Explain how prayer could support a person's belief in God.

4. With a partner consider how the faith of people who are not healed at Lourdes might be affected.

1 How did it all begin?

AIM

To understand how the appearance of the world may lead some people to believe in God and others to reach a non-religious conclusion.

KEY TERMS

causation argument the idea that everything has been caused (started off) by something else
design argument when things are connected and seem to have a purpose, e.g. the eye is designed for seeing

STARTER

Think of a designer garment. Make a list of the features that show that this item was produced by a high-quality designer.

The design argument

William Paley put forward the **design argument** several hundred years ago. He said if somebody happened to find a watch and had never seen one before in their life, they would be astounded. The fact that something so tiny had such an intricate mechanism would lead them to believe that it had been made by a very clever person. Nothing like that could possibly happen by accident. Paley said the same argument could be applied to the universe, which is far more complicated than any watch mechanism. It could never have happened by chance, it must have been designed by an extremely clever being. The only possible designer is God. That proves God exists, he reasoned.

ACTIVITY

1. What do you think Paley would say if someone asked him about the reason for earthquakes?

The causation argument

If something unexpected happens we always try to see what has caused it. If a jug falls off the table, or a car veers across the road, most people look for the cause of that action. 'Things do not happen by themselves', they say.

The **causation argument** says that the mere existence of the universe is proof God exists. If the universe had a beginning then something must have caused it. The universe did not happen by accident and only something as powerful as God could have brought it into existence. That proves God exists.

ACTIVITY

2. Working with a partner, try to come up with three things that might happen without anyone or anything causing them. Share your ideas with the class.

The argument for the Big Bang

This widely accepted scientific theory for the beginning of the universe states that around fifteen billion years ago there was a cosmic explosion – a 'Big Bang'. Gases and matter were thrown apart at virtually the speed of light. Our universe was formed as gases cooled. Support for this theory is found in the way the galaxies are continuing to move away from each other and that echoes of the Big Bang can be picked up today by powerful radio telescopes.

ACTIVITY

3. What would the supporters of the causation argument say about the Big Bang theory?

Figure F *Scientists have worked out that this is the model of DNA, the structure of life. Many people think our understanding of DNA is the most important discovery of the past hundred years. We would never have known of its existence without scientists, but they did not invent DNA. It has always been there since the beginning of time. Did DNA happen by chance?*

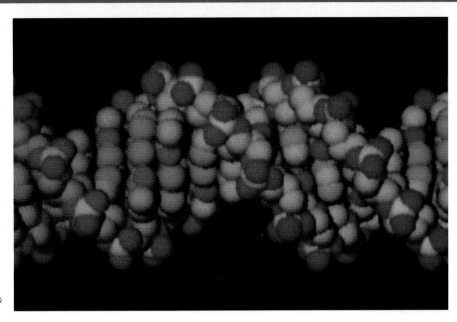

The argument for natural selection

Darwin's theory of evolution by natural selection states that over millions of years plant and animal life has adapted to its environment. Plants and animals were not necessarily created in the form we see them today. They have evolved and continue to do so. Each adaptation is passed on to their offspring and those organisms that fail to change simply die out. Only the species which are the fittest and best suited to the changing conditions on the planet will survive.

For discussion

'Some people say you cannot believe in evolution and God. Well I think that God has to use evolution to create intelligent life. Humans have got to think for themselves or they would just be programmed like mini computers.' As a class discuss the point this scientist is making.

FOR RESEARCH

- List four ways in which we use DNA today.
- Work out why our knowledge of DNA might lead some people to believe in the existence of God.
- Work out why our knowledge of DNA might lead other people to conclude that God does not exist.
- Does a person's DNA tell you everything you need to know about them?

ACTIVITY

4. a) Write down your thoughts on why each of the arguments on this spread might lead some people to believe in God.

b) Look at each argument again and decide why it might lead an atheist to say God does not exist.

c) How would an agnostic react to each of the arguments?

AIM

To understand why the existence of evil and suffering can cause problems for those who believe in God and lead some people to question or reject belief in God.

KEY TERMS

moral evil actions done by humans which cause suffering

natural evil things which cause suffering but have nothing to do with humans, e.g. earthquakes

STARTER

With a partner look at Figures G and H. What differences are there between these forms of suffering? Who might be to blame in each case? Could either of them have been avoided?

(photograph posed by models © Matt Harris)

Figure G *Most people think that hurting children is one of the worst forms of moral evil. Why is hurting a child worse than hurting an adult?*

The big problem

One of the difficulties people have when they consider whether God exists or not is understanding why suffering happens. For people who have prayed for help but not seen any response, this might be proof that God does not exist.

Moral evil

Moral evil is suffering caused by people. The suffering in Figure G is caused by someone who knows what they are doing and intends to cause harm. A religious believer might find it difficult to understand why God created people who were capable of doing such evil. Moral evil can also happen accidentally. The driver who falls asleep at the wheel and crashes into children walking along the pavement causes great suffering.

ACTIVITY

1. List four more situations you would say involve moral evil.

What is the problem?

When cases of child cruelty come to light people immediately start asking questions and try to apportion blame. The usual questions are 'Who did this?' and 'Why did it happen?' Some people might ask a deeper question about why God allows such things to happen. If you look back to page 9 you will notice that God is described as benevolent, omniscient and omnipotent.

- Believers find it hard to understand how a God who is said to be benevolent (in other words good and kind) can allow suffering to happen to people.
- Some suggest that perhaps the answer is that God is not omnipotent after all. Perhaps God is not powerful enough to prevent evil happening.

Figure H *This devastation was caused by the tsunami on 26 December 2004. An earthquake in the Indian Ocean caused tidal waves of such size and force that people living near the coast could not escape. At least 225,000 people are estimated to have died that day across 11 nations, making it the worse natural disaster in history.*

- Other people question whether God really is omniscient. They say if God does know everything about the past, present and future, then God would have known this was going to happen and could have stopped it.
- People who are faithful believers, and communicate with God through prayer, might wonder why their prayers have gone unanswered when this sort of thing happens.
- If God created everything in the universe, did God create evil?
- An atheist might argue that these events happen because God does not exist at all.

Natural evil

Natural evil is, as the name suggests, caused by nature. Some people argue that, terrible though it is, natural evil is not a form of evil. It is simply suffering which is caused by a natural occurrence. It might take the form of an earthquake, volcanic eruption, drought or tidal wave. It can often result in widespread suffering when people are injured and made homeless by a disaster. Believers find it hard to understand why such disasters happen to innocent people.

⚲ For discussion

Look at the problems highlighted by bullet points on these pages and decide how many also apply to natural evil.

ACTIVITIES

2. a) Divide your page into two columns. In one note down the argument in favour of a designer God. In the other note down the case against a designer God based on natural evil.

b) Underneath write one sentence stating whether you think the existence of evil and suffering leads you to believe or disbelieve in God.

c) Write a final sentence explaining why you have come to that conclusion.

3. Either watch the national and local news on television one evening and note down all the stories which involve suffering, or go through a copy of a newspaper and cut out ten stories that involve suffering.

4. Sort your stories into instances of moral evil and natural evil. Not every situation is clearly one or the other. Some cases of suffering may be a mixture of the two. War, for example, which might be a moral evil, could lead to a crop failure in the region and a famine. Go through each and decide who, or what, caused the incident and whether it could have been avoided.

PATH TO THE TOP

With a partner consider what the difference between evil and suffering might be. Try to answer these questions.

- Does evil always cause suffering?
- Is suffering always evil? (It might be helpful to think about a weight-lifter training for the Olympics before you answer this one.)

1 The Christian response to evil and suffering

To understand how Christians respond to the problems of evil and suffering.

KEY TERM

prayer an attempt to contact God, usually through words

STARTER

As a class, brainstorm the problems that evil and suffering cause religious believers.

What do Christians believe are the reasons for evil and suffering?

Christians differ in their views about the causes of evil and suffering.

- Some believe that God created a perfect world for humanity, but Adam and Eve used their free will to disobey God. Their punishment resulted in humans being separated from God. This has led to suffering and evil. God sent Jesus to die for the sins of humanity, rise again, and bring people back to God.
- Others believe God created people with free will and because people are not programmed like computers, they can choose whether to do good or evil. When they choose evil, suffering occurs.
- To some Christians, life is a test. The way people react to suffering and evil determines whether they go to **heaven** or **hell** in the afterlife (see pages 26–7).
- Others say that God does have reasons for permitting suffering and evil, but humans cannot hope to understand the mind of God.

How do Christians respond to the problem of suffering?

Christians are guided by Jesus when they consider how to respond to suffering. Jesus, according to Christians, is the Son of God, and lived the life of a human being on earth, experiencing suffering and death. This shows Christians that God understands their suffering and has not left them alone, but shares in their sufferings. For Christians, the shape of the cross on which Jesus was crucified is a potent symbol of their faith. It means that good will eventually triumph over evil as it did when Jesus rose from the dead on the third day. Christians also believe that no matter how much they suffer in this life, they will be rewarded by eternal life in heaven.

Following Jesus' example

Jesus taught his followers to use prayer to ask for God's help. Jesus prayed to God his father for strength to face the evil that would kill him. **Intercession** is the name given to prayers in which Christians ask God's help for those who are suffering. Christians accept that some of their prayers may appear to go unanswered, but they argue that it is not because God does not care, or does not exist. God has his own way of dealing with our intercessions which people do not understand. It is also possible that God will answer the prayers of the faithful in unexpected ways.

Jesus also taught his followers to be of service to those who are suffering. During his time on earth, Jesus helped the sick and dying and taught his followers to copy his example. Christians today help relieve suffering by donating money to charities who can bring professional help in times of need. Other Christians take a more active role by giving their time or expertise to relieve suffering. This might range from collecting money for a good cause, to working as a volunteer in a hospital or travelling abroad to help in a disaster area.

There is a story in the Bible which Jesus told when he was asked who would go to heaven and who would go to hell. He said that God would divide people into two groups, just as a shepherd separates his flock into sheep and goats. Only those people who had personally shown compassion towards Jesus could enter the kingdom of heaven, he told them. When his followers were confused by this Jesus explained.

I was hungry and you fed me, thirsty and you gave me a drink; I was a stranger and you received me in your homes, naked and you clothed me; I was sick and you took care of me, in prison and you visited me... I tell you whenever you did this for one of the least important of these brothers of mine you did it for me! (Matthew 25: 35–6, 40)

ACTIVITIES

1. 'Suffering has a purpose,' said the 400-metre Olympic hopeful during training. With a partner discuss what the sprinter meant. Compare his view of suffering with the Christian attitude towards suffering.
2. Make a list of five ways in which a modern Christian could follow Jesus' example of fighting evil or relieving suffering.

For discussion
'A benevolent God could not possibly allow suffering.' Do you agree? Would a Christian agree with this? Why?

Figure I Some Christians give service to others. The Christians running this soup kitchen belong to the Religious Society of Friends (Quakers). They are giving their time voluntarily to help relieve the suffering of the homeless at Christmas by providing them with hot food and shelter.

ACTIVITIES

3. Cut out a picture of natural evil and another of moral evil from a newspaper or magazine. Stick each picture in the centre of a plain A4 sheet of card or paper to make a poster. Label the natural evil and the moral evil. Write on your poster what a Christian might say about the suffering in your picture. Include a quotation from a sacred text if you can.
4. What would a Christian say is the connection between the words of Jesus and Figure I?

1 Putting it all together

ACTIVITIES

1. Visit www.heinemann.co.uk/hotlinks, type in the express code 2280P and click on this section to discover details about how one Christian denomination, such as Quakers or the Baptist Church, work to relieve suffering in the world. Write a brief account of what they do, then explain why Christians believe they should do this.

2. Find out more about the religious experiences some Christians claim to have had from a pilgrimage to Lourdes by visiting www.heinemann.co.uk/hotlinks, typing in the express code 2280P and clicking on this section. How might these experiences support a belief in God?

3. Make an A3 poster that demonstrates the causation argument. Include in your poster a panel explaining clearly why this argument might lead some people to believe in God.

4. You have been asked to prepare the opening questions for a celebrity interviewer in a television chat show. One of his guests is a well-known Christian astronomer and the other a space technician from NASA who is an atheist. The interviewer needs to get his guests arguing. Give him three questions to start things off.

5. Sort these arguments into two columns. Head one column 'Arguments to support a belief in God'. Head the other column 'Arguments against the existence of God'.

- Miracles are just illusions. Science will soon be able to prove that.
- Miracles do occur and God is the only satisfactory explanation for this.
- If God is supposed to be good and powerful why does he not heal everybody who is sick, rather than just performing a few miracle cures?
- Personal religious experiences are all in the mind; there is no God.
- Personal religious experiences are all in the mind, which is where God communicates with believers.
- Miracles are one way in which God answers the prayers of believers.
- Miracles are just another name for luck or coincidence.

Tackling an exam question

Here is a **(b)** question from the exam paper.

> Outline the view that evil and suffering are a problem for religious believers. **(6)**

Planning your answer to this question

1. Go through and underline the important words in this question. This will focus your mind and stop you wandering off the point: <u>Outline</u>, <u>evil and suffering</u>, <u>problem for religious believers</u>.

HINT
Pages 16–17 will refresh your memory on this subject. The **(b)** question is asking you to give facts and then show how they apply to a religion. Make sure you refer to Christianity when answering this question.

2. Analyse the question. <u>Evil and suffering</u> and <u>problem</u> are key terms in this question. The question is asking you to outline what problems they cause. Do not go into great detail; just get the main points down. As part of your planning for this answer go back to pages 16–17 and list the points a religious believer is going to be concerned about.

3. <u>Religious believers</u> are also important to this question, so you need to be clear why they, more than non-believers, are going to have problems with evil and suffering. In what ways does the existence of evil challenge the beliefs of religious people?

4. Note down any key terms that appeared in this part of the specification. If you can use some specialist terms in your answer it might raise your level because it shows you have a good understanding of the issue.

Student's answer

Lots of people say God doesn't exist because of all the terrible things that happen in the world. I think they are wrong. It is people that get the guns and shoot innocent people outside clubs. You can't blame God for that. Then there are floods which kill people. Who started them? I do not believe in God so I wouldn't say it was him. ✓ (Level 1)

Examiner's comments

The student clearly did not sort out the important parts of this question. The answer started off well with a good example of relevant information in his first sentence, but then he wandered off the point. The answer lacks structure and the student has even given things he was not asked for, such as his opinion of the problem! This answer does not get beyond Level 1. To improve his answer, the student needs to briefly say how a Christian would react to evil and suffering. Then he must link this to the believer's view of God and explain why this might cause a problem.

Level 1 (2 marks)

For an isolated example of relevant knowledge.

Level 2 (4 marks)

For basic relevant knowledge presented within a limited structure.

Level 3 (6 marks)

For an organised outline/description using relevant knowledge with limited use of specialist vocabulary.

Student's improved answer

Lots of people say God doesn't exist because of all the terrible things that happen in the world. Christians believe that God is benevolent so they might find it difficult to understand why a God who loves people would allow suffering to happen. ✓ (L1)

Many religious believers who think God is omniscient and omnipotent would not be able to understand why God doesn't stop evil when he knows it is going to happen. ✓ (L2)

Believers who have prayed to God to help them through their suffering would also find it hard to understand why their prayers weren't answered. ✓ (L3)

1 **a)** A clear definition is required (see p. 6).

b) Pages 8–11 will help you.

c) Remember to say what the religious experiences might be **and** how they affect a person's belief in God (see pp. 12–13). There are two parts to this answer! Help with this sort of question appears on page 122.

d) This is your chance to give a personal opinion. Say what you think and why. Then say what other people think and why they say it. Pages 14–15 will help with scientific ideas and page 123 will help with this sort of argumentative answer. Make sure you come to a conclusion.

Questions 1(b) and 2(b) are taken from Edexcel Unit B paper 2004. Questions 1(c) and 2(d) are based on questions from the Edexcel Unit B Specimen Paper.

SECTION ONE: BELIEVING IN GOD

You must answer ONE question from this section.

Leave blank

EITHER QUESTION 1

1 **a)** What does *atheism* mean? **(2)**

b) Describe the main features of a Christian upbringing. **(6)**

c) Explain why religious experiences might lead to or support a belief in God. **(8)**

d) *'Modern science makes it impossible to believe in God.'*

Do you agree? Give reasons for your opinion, showing you have considered another point of view. **(4)**

(Total 20 marks) Q1

OR QUESTION 2

2 **a)** What does *conversion* mean? **(2)**

b) Outline an argument for God's existence based on the appearance of design in the world. **(6)**

c) Explain why the existence of evil and suffering in the world leads some people to become atheists. **(8)**

d) *'Children should be allowed to make up their own minds about whether to believe in God or not.'*

Do you agree? Give reasons for your answer showing you have considered another point of view. **(4)** Q2

(Total 20 marks)

---

2 **a)** Keep your definition brief (see p. 12).

b) Be concise (no waffle) but get all the points down (see pp. 14–15).

c) There are two parts to this answer. First state the problem, then the effect that it has on some people's beliefs (see pp. 16–17). Page 122 gives help with **(c)** questions.

d) Your views are required so you could begin 'I think … because …' Then give the other side's views 'Other people think … because …' You must come to a conclusion (which could be that you are not sure) showing you have considered another viewpoint. See page 123 for help with **(d)** questions.

2 MATTERS OF LIFE AND DEATH

In this chapter you will learn:

- about differences among Christians in their attitudes towards life after death, including resurrection, immortality of the soul, purgatory and heaven and hell
- why Christians believe in life after death
- why people of no specific religion believe in life after death, including near-death experiences and the paranormal
- why some people do not believe in life after death
- about Christian teachings on the sanctity of life (Genesis 1, Exodus 20: 13, Romans 14: 8, 1 Corinthians 6: 19) and statements by the Churches
- about the nature of abortion including current British legislation and non-religious arguments concerning abortion
- about differences among Christians in their attitudes to contraception and the reasons for them
- about Christian attitudes to abortion and euthanasia and the reasons for them
- about the nature of euthanasia (assisted suicide, voluntary and non-voluntary euthanasia), current British legislation and arguments concerning euthanasia.

Figure A *Paramedics face life and death situations on a daily basis. Do you think they would be helped by a belief in God? Why?*

The key terms you must know are:

resurrection, immortality of the soul, purgatory, heaven, hell, paranormal, sanctity of life, abortion, contraception, euthanasia, assisted suicide, voluntary euthanasia, non-voluntary euthanasia

ACTIVITY

1. Look at Figure A above. With a partner, discuss whether you think it is always right to try to resuscitate a very sick patient. Explain your answer. Are there any situations where you think preserving life at all costs is questionable? Why?

AIM

To understand and evaluate the arguments for and against a belief in life after death.

KEY TERM

paranormal unexplained things which are thought to have spiritual causes, e.g. ghosts and mediums

STARTER

Look back to pages 6 and 7 and the definitions of atheism, agnosticism and believer in the glossary. Decide what each person would say about the idea of life after death.

A recent survey in Britain showed that 70 per cent of the population thought there was some sort of life after death. Interestingly, the majority of those questioned did not belong to any religion.

The case for life after death

- People have experienced paranormal activities, i.e. things which are thought to have a supernatural cause.
- Mind over matter – the mind can make the body do impossible things, such as walk barefoot over red hot coals without getting burnt. On occasions the mind can persuade the body to heal itself of an 'incurable' illness. Scientists agree that the brain is extremely powerful and we do not fully understand how it works.
- The brain is separate from the body. For instance, we can imagine all sorts of conflicting emotions in the mind that we have never experienced. Also, the body can live on after the mind is dead, e.g. a person on a life-support machine can be brain-dead.
- People from all parts of the world and from all sorts of religions, as well as those with no religion at all, have believed in life after death since earliest times. Are they all wrong?

Figure B *The Victorians used trick photography to try to convince people that there was life after death. Do you think science could ever be used to prove, or disprove, something supernatural? Why? Do you think that if you believe in life after death, you have to believe in ghosts?*

Paranormal experiences

- Near-death experiences – these have been reported in cases where a patient was pronounced clinically dead for a brief time, then revived. Such people tell of remarkably similar experiences such as travelling through a tunnel towards a bright light and peace. Usually they never reach the light because they are revived and have to return to life. Most who have had this experience said they did not want to come back to earth. Often their experience profoundly changed their attitude to life. They were convinced they had seen evidence of the existence of God and of life after death so they no longer feared death.

- There is a widespread belief in the existence of ghosts, who are thought to be the spirits of dead people that are sometimes visible to the living. Ghosts seem to be there for a purpose. Some haunt the living, some are said to give warnings and others just wander around without making contact with the living.

What do you think about this?

One suggestion is that that our brain is like a computer which operates the human body. It is powered by an energy force you could call the mind. This energy is separate from the brain in the same way that electricity is separate from the computer it operates. Switch a computer off and it goes dead, but the electricity is still there even if it is not being used. Do you think this image could be applied to the human brain? Could there be an energy force which continues to exist after the body has died?

The case against life after death

- Scientific evidence shows that when the body dies, everything decays.
- No one has returned from the dead to tell us.
- The end of life means exactly that. It is illogical to speak about life after death.
- Life-support machines prove the brain dies before the body.

The case against the paranormal

Those who disagree with the idea of the paranormal believe that it is all imagination. People who desperately wish to make contact with someone they loved who has died probably knew them well enough to be able to visualise their presence and know what they might say.

Stories of near-death experiences are similar because they are hallucinations conjured up by a dying brain as it closes down. They are simply a chemical reaction to oxygen starvation. It is similar to a computer going through various closing-down functions as it is switched off. It is also well known that some drugs given to patients undergoing surgery can produce weird dreams.

The US Navy conducted experiments to find out how much gravitational force their pilots could withstand before they passed out. Several reported that just before they lost consciousness they experienced tunnel vision, saw bright lights and felt a sense of exhilaration. One major difference, however, was that none of the pilots were changed by their experience nor felt it was evidence of life after death.

ACTIVITIES

1. Divide your page into two columns. List arguments for and against a belief in life after death. Prepare a presentation to show the contrasting views people hold. Include the atheist's view. You could use PowerPoint to display your presentation.

2. What would you ask a person claiming to have had a near-death experience if they were appearing on a television chat show? Why do you think viewers would be interested in their experience?

AIM

To understand why Christians believe in life after death.

KEY TERMS

heaven a place of paradise where God rules

hell a place of horrors where Satan rules

immortality of the soul the idea that the soul lives on after the death of the body

resurrection the belief that, after death, the body stays in the grave until the end of the world when it is raised

Reasons why Christians believe in life after death

The resurrection of Jesus

Because Jesus became human and suffered death but then rose from the dead, Christians are convinced there is life after death. By dying Jesus paid the price for all the sins committed by people in the world. This means people can be forgiven and will have an eternal life with God. Some time after his **resurrection** Jesus returned to heaven and this leads Christians to believe heaven exists.

STARTER

Look at Figure C and look up Luke 24: 37–9. How did Jesus explain to his followers that he was a bodily resurrection and not a ghostly apparition? Do you think the artist intended the picture to show exactly what happened? What might people mean when they say the picture is symbolic?

Figure C 'The Resurrection' by Piero Della Francesco. The resurrection of Jesus is the single most important reason why Christians believe in the life after death.

What the scriptures teach

There are many passages in the New Testament confirming that there is life after death. Jesus explained to his followers on several occasions that those who believed in him would have everlasting life in heaven.

Here he tells them that they will die, but if they trust in Jesus they will be brought back to life. 'Jesus said, "I am the resurrection and the life; he who believes in me, though he die, yet shall he live".' (John 11: 25)

Once again Jesus tells them that the key to eternal life is belief in him. 'For God loved the world so much that he gave his only Son, so that everyone who believes in him may not die but have eternal life. For God did not send his Son into the world to be its judge, but to be its saviour.' (John 3: 16–17)

St Paul, who came later, wrote to early Christians who were unsure about life after death. He explained, 'But the truth is that Christ has been raised from death, as the guarantee that those who sleep in death will also be raised'. When St Paul was challenged by someone who asked, 'How can the dead be raised to life? What kind of body will they have?' St Paul replied, 'You fool! When you sow a seed in the ground, it does not sprout to life unless it dies. And what you sow is a bare seed, perhaps a grain of wheat or some other grain, not the full-bodied plant that will later grow up. God provides that seed with the body he wishes; he gives each seed its own proper body… That is how it will be when the dead are raised to life. When the body is buried, it is mortal; when raised, it will be immortal. When buried, it is ugly and weak; when raised, it is beautiful and strong. When buried, it is a physical body; when raised, it will be a spiritual body. There is, of course, a physical body, so there has to be a spiritual body.' (1 Corinthians 15: 20, 35–8, 42–4)

What the Christian Church teaches

Because Christians through the ages have been convinced that there is life after death, this forms an essential part of Church teachings. Christians know that their physical body will die, but they are certain that is not the end. They have faith that sometime after death there will be a Day of Judgement when people will be brought back to life to go before God and have their earthly deeds judged. Christians call this return to life resurrection.

Although their physical body dies, Christians are convinced that their soul continues to exist in eternity with God. They call this belief the **immortality of the soul**.

The Bible refers to the belief in life after death as essential for Christians. Many of the churches have the following statement in their **creed**, which makes it an essential belief for Christians. 'I believe in the resurrection of the body and the life everlasting.'

In addition, many Christians find the idea of life after death perfectly logical. Without it, they say, life would be pointless. Some Christians also accept evidence of near-death experiences and the paranormal as further proof of life after death.

ACTIVITIES

1. Write a paragraph that could be displayed on a panel with the painting in Figure C. Explain what is going on and its significance to Christians.

2. St Paul says that a dead body is like a seed. Explain what he means by that analogy.

3. Write a paragraph explaining how the resurrection of Jesus is linked with the Christian belief in life after death.

AIM

To understand the different attitudes among Christians to life after death and the reasons for them.

Christian beliefs

Although Christians believe that there is life after death, and that they will be judged on their actions, they differ in their understanding of the form life after death will take. Some believe in resurrection (see page 26), some believe in the immortality of the soul (see page 27), and some accept both beliefs. Here are some of the most widely held views and the reasons for them.

Resurrection

Some Christians believe that after death the body stays in the grave until the Day of Judgement. Then everyone will be raised from the dead and brought before God for judgement. The good will go to heaven for eternity; sinners who have never repented will go to hell for eternity.

Reasons for this belief

- Jesus' body was raised from the dead.
- The Creed says 'I believe in the resurrection of the body and the life everlasting'.
- St Paul teaches this belief (see page 27).

Immortality of the soul

Some Christians believe that after death the body will stay in the grave, but the soul will be taken straight to God for judgement. People who have led a pure life will stay with God. There is a difference of opinion about the fate of sinners. Some believe they will be sent to hell, others think there is no such place. Separation from God is hell.

Reasons for this belief

- Jesus told the thief crucified alongside him, 'I promise you that today you will be in Paradise with me'. (Luke 23: 43)
- Jesus also told his followers, 'There are many rooms in my Father's house, and I am going to prepare a place for you. I will come back and take you to myself, so that you will be where I am'. (John 14: 1–3)
- The Creed states 'I believe in the **communion of saints**' which means that the souls of dead saints continue to live.
- For some people a paranormal experience, such as seeing ghosts, is proof of the immortality of the soul.
- Others say that the teaching of the Bible is the only evidence needed for the immortality of the soul.

Roman Catholic beliefs

Roman Catholics believe both in resurrection and in the immortality of the soul. After death the souls of those who have led pure lives will go straight to heaven. Those who have sinned go into a state of waiting and preparation for heaven where their souls will be cleansed. This state is called **purgatory**. People who have committed great evil and never repented will go to hell for eternity. On the Last Day, Jesus will return to earth and raise the dead from their graves and reunite them with their souls. Then God will judge everyone.

Reasons for this belief

- Jesus rose from the dead.
- The Creed states that Jesus rose again on the third day and 'is seated at the right hand of the Father and will come again to judge the living and the dead'.

Figure D *'Judgement Day' by Fra Angelico. This very large, fifteenth century painting shows the medieval idea of life after death. God sits on high surrounded by angels and saints, dividing humanity into those going to heaven and those going to hell. The centre path is made of graves that have opened. Look at the landscapes of heaven and hell. What is happening to the people? How do you think these images might have made people feel or behave?*

- The Bible says 'For God loved the world so much that he gave his only Son, so that everyone who believes in him may not die but have eternal life'. (John 3: 16–17)
- The Catechism teaches these beliefs.
- Purgatory makes sense of immortality and resurrection.

PATH TO THE TOP

The **communion of saints** is a useful concept. 'Communion' in this context means community and the word 'saints' is used to mean all Christians, alive or dead, living on earth and in heaven. Some Christians believe it is possible for those on earth to pray to those in heaven to ask for guidance, or to ask them to speak to God.

HINT

Remember there is a wide variation in Christian beliefs about this subject. For instance, some Christians would not accept material about the paranormal as evidence of life after death. Not all Christians believe in the existence of hell either, because they say a loving God would never allow such evil to exist. To be on the safe side, always say 'Some Christians believe…'.

ACTIVITIES

1. What is the difference between resurrection and immortality of the soul?

2. Present the different Christian interpretations of life after death as a diagram that you could use to help you revise.

3. Which view of life after death do you think the artist of the painting in Figure D was depicting? What is the evidence for this?

AIM

To understand the British law on abortion and different attitudes towards it.

KEY TERM

abortion the removal of a foetus from the womb before it can survive

Figure E Under British law a foetus can be aborted up until 24 weeks into the pregnancy. If a scan reveals that the child is likely to be born severely physically or mentally handicapped, doctors may advise parents to abort the foetus. What would you do in such a situation? Should issues like this be decided in court?

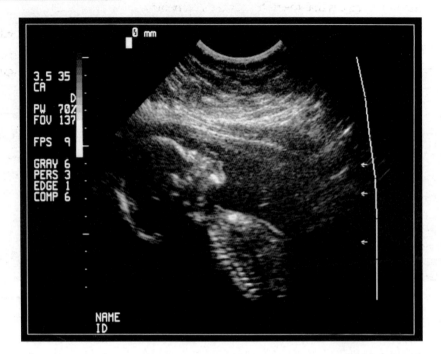

What does the law say about abortion?

In 1967 a law was passed to permit **abortions** in the UK if two doctors agreed that either:

- the mother's life was at risk
- the mother's physical or mental health would suffer
- the child was likely to be born severely physically or mentally handicapped
- there would be a seriously bad effect on other children in the family.

The Act was amended in 1990 to prevent abortions being carried out after 24 weeks of pregnancy. This was because some babies born prematurely after 24 weeks have survived.

ACTIVITY

1. Create a fact file in your exercise book concerning the British law on abortion.

The abortion debate

In spring 2005, some people said that advances in medical science and the huge number of abortions that take place every day (around 500 per day in England) meant that the issue had to be examined again.

New hi-tech ultra-sound images of foetuses in the womb have shown that at 12 weeks the baby is beginning to make walking motions, at 14 weeks it can suck its thumb and yawn and at 18 weeks it is opening its eyes. With better incubators and medical care, premature babies of 23 weeks are now surviving and there have even been a few cases of 22 week babies surviving. The abortion debate was further fuelled when one leading medical expert stated that the technology now exists to diagnose handicaps in a foetus before 20 weeks so there is no need for late abortions.

When does life begin?

Many arguments about abortion hinge on this crucial question. Some people would say a foetus is a life. The reason they give is that the foetus contains everything necessary (the full DNA) to make an individual human being. Once a sperm and an egg fuse, a new life begins. That life has the right to exist.

Others disagree, saying that the fusion of a sperm and an egg is no more than a biological reaction, but that at some point during the development of the fertilised egg, life begins. The big question, of course, is when? Is it when the heart begins to beat or when the baby first moves?

Some religions say life begins at the point God puts a soul into the foetus. But when is that?

Some people think that a foetus should only be recognised as an independent person when it is capable of surviving outside the mother's body.

ACTIVITY

2. With a partner consider whether any of the arguments above would be affected by advances in medical science such as developments in ultra-sound scans and hi-tech incubators. When would you say life begins? Why?

PATH TO THE TOP

Use appropriate terms to boost your grade. The following is worth learning:

- **doctrine of double effect** the idea that deciding to perform one action can trigger another. For example, a woman might receive treatment for cancer of the womb that, in the process, kills her unborn child. This would not be classed as an abortion because the doctor set out to cure the cancer, not to cause an abortion.

Arguments in favour of abortion

- A woman has the right to choose; it is her body, her life, her future and her child.
- A child's quality of life is important. If a baby is going to lead a miserable life because it is not wanted, or a painful life because of severe disabilities, then it might be kinder to prevent the child ever being born.
- A mother's health and welfare are more important than her unborn child's.
- There are too many people on the planet, and abortion controls population growth.

Arguments against abortion

- Abortion is a form of murder.
- Everyone has the right to be born so they can fulfil their potential.
- All life has value.
- A foetus does have rights and, because it cannot speak for itself, the law must protect it.
- Life is a sacred gift from God and only God can end a pregnancy (see pages 34–5 for more detail on the sanctity of life argument).

ACTIVITY

3. Role-play the discussion between a teenage girl, who wants an abortion because her pregnancy was an accident, and her boyfriend, who believes strongly that abortion is wrong. He wants her to have the baby, which he will look after.

For discussion

'The life of the mother is always worth more than that of her unborn child.' Would you agree with this statement? Are there any exceptions? Is it a mother's right to be free to go out and have a good time or to get a better job?

2 Euthanasia

AIM

To understand the British law on euthanasia and the different attitudes towards it.

KEY TERMS

assisted suicide providing a seriously ill person with the means to commit suicide

euthanasia an easy and gentle death

non-voluntary euthanasia ending someone's life painlessly when they are unable to ask, but you have good reason for thinking they would want you to do so, e.g. switching off a life-support machine

voluntary euthanasia the situation where someone dying in pain asks a doctor to end her/his life painlessly

STARTER

Discuss with a partner whether you think a person who is terminally ill has the right to end their life? Is it fair to ask someone else to do it for them?

Euthanasia in Britain

Although it is generally acknowledged that **euthanasia** is illegal in Britain, there is no specific law forbidding it, but there are laws that forbid murder.

Advances in medical science have brought the issue of euthanasia to the fore because better drugs and more sophisticated machines can prolong life. Some people claim this is not always in the patient's best interests, particularly if their quality of life is poor. There have been several court cases where doctors have requested permission to switch off the life-support machine of a person who is already brain-dead.

ACTIVITY

1. With a partner consider the different forms of euthanasia in the boxes below and decide which ones some people might argue are not actually murder.

Euthanasia

The word comes from the Greek where *eu* = good and *thanasis* = death. Some people refer to euthanasia as 'mercy killing', because it involves ending someone's life painlessly at their request, in order to prevent further suffering.

Voluntary euthanasia

This is also called **assisted suicide** because someone, such as a doctor, deliberately ends a person's life at his or her request. It might be by administering an overdose of drugs or deliberately leaving strong drugs within reach of the patient knowing what they want to do. If the patient subsequently commits suicide then the doctor is considered to have assisted in that suicide.

Passive euthanasia

This is where a patient is allowed to die. A seriously ill cancer patient may not be revived if they collapse from a heart attack or a severely deformed baby is not put on a life-support machine. In some situations a patient may be given strong drugs to control their pain, and these may hasten their death.

Non-voluntary euthanasia

This is when a person helps somebody die without consulting them because the patient is in no position to make their wishes known. The most obvious situation would be switching off the life-support machine of a patient who is 'brain-dead'.

Use appropriate terms to boost your grade. The following is worth learning:

- **doctrine of double effect** this involves a doctor treating a person for an illness knowing that the treatment might actually shorten the patient's life. This is not classed as murder.

Arguments in favour of euthanasia

- Suicide is legal, so why not help someone who cannot commit suicide themselves.

Figure F *Diane Pretty, who suffered from a terminal illness, asked the British court's permission for her husband to help her to die because she was in great pain. She did not want him to be prosecuted for murder. When she lost her case she went to the European Court of Human Justice where once again she lost. Do you think that was the correct verdict? Why?*

- If an animal were suffering, we would have it put down because it is the humane thing to do.
- It costs a lot of money to keep people alive when there is no hope for them, that money could be better spent on those who can get better.
- It is their life; they should have the right to end it if they want.
- Someone in great pain has no quality of life, so they should be able to end it in a dignified manner if they wish.
- It is not fair on the relatives to have to watch their loved one dying painfully.

Arguments against euthanasia

- Drugs can be used to control pain.
- Euthanasia is just a fancy name for murder.
- People who ask for euthanasia are often depressed and not in the right state of mind to make such an important decision.
- Some people, like elderly relatives, might be pressurised by their family to stop being a nuisance and seek euthanasia.
- Doctors take an oath to save life, it is wrong to ask them to kill people. People would be scared to go to the doctor if euthanasia was an option.
- A doctor's diagnosis can be wrong. People can get better or medical science might find a cure for them.

ACTIVITY

2. Look back to page 23. What connection does Figure A have with the issue on these pages? Would your answer to the question in the activity box on page 23 be any different now?

For discussion

As a class debate this issue: 'Euthanasia should be legalised in the UK'. Make a note of the main arguments put forward by each side. Which side do you support and why?

2 Christian attitudes to the sanctity of life and to euthanasia

AIM

To understand Christian teachings about the sanctity of life and how these might apply to abortion and euthanasia.

KEY TERM

sanctity of life the belief that life is holy and belongs to God

The sanctity of life

Christians believe that God created everything and humans were created in God's own image. This makes life holy or sanctified. Christians regard life as a gift from God which they are loaned but do not own. That means they cannot dispose of life as they wish. To emphasise God's special relationship with people, God became human in the person of Jesus. Because Jesus accepted his suffering and never tried to escape from it, Christians believe it teaches them to cherish and preserve life.

The Bible says:

Don't you know that your body is the temple of the Holy Spirit, who lives in you and who was given to you by God? You do not belong to yourselves but to God. (1 Corinthians 6: 19)

God created human beings, making them to be like himself. (Genesis 1: 27)

Do not commit murder. (1 Exodus 20: 13)

None of us lives for himself only, none of us dies for himself only. If we live, it is for the Lord that we live, and if we die, it is for the Lord that we die. (Romans 14: 7–8)

Based on these and other teachings, the Churches state clearly their belief that all life is sacred. Look at the role God plays in the extracts above.

The Methodist Church says:

Christians believe that human beings are created in God's image. All human life should therefore be reverenced. (What the Churches say on moral and social issues, 3rd edn, CEM, 2000)

The Orthodox Church says:

Orthodox Christians profess that all life comes from God and that human life represents his most precious gift. (What the Churches say on moral and social issues, 3rd edn, CEM, 2000)

The Church of England says:

All human life, including life developed in the womb, is created by God in his own image and is therefore to be nurtured, supported and protected. (What the Churches say on moral and social issues, 3rd edn, CEM, 2000)

ACTIVITY

1. Read the Christian teachings on the **sanctity of life** and compare them with the statements by the Churches. What message is coming from all of them? What reason is given for this message?

Christian attitudes to euthanasia

Christians are agreed that God, the creator of life, is the only one who can end life. This means that euthanasia is a grave sin. Christians differ in their opinions over whether medical science can intervene.

- Some Christians accept that doctors can give drugs to relieve suffering even if this shortens a patient's life.
- Christians are divided on the issue of switching off life-support machines. Many believe it is acceptable if the patient is already brain-dead.

- Some Christians believe doctors should not carry out expensive treatments that only prolong a poor quality of life but do not aid recovery.
- There are other Christians who say life is precious and everything should be done to prolong it.

The Baptist Union

The Baptist Union says that, in principle, they are opposed to anything that removes life, 'because life is God's gift and because any relationship is worth preserving, however poor or shallow it may be' (*What the Churches say on moral and social issues*, 3rd edn, CEM, 2000). However, they accept that when a person is 'brain-dead' and unable to maintain a relationship of any kind with friends or relatives and where medical opinion states there is no hope of recovery, it would be acceptable to withdraw treatment.

The Roman Catholic Church

The Roman Catholic Church says 'Our time on earth is a pilgrimage of faith – it is not for a person themselves, or anyone else, with or without consent, to interrupt this journey before God calls him or her from this world to the life after death' (*What the Churches say on moral and social issues*, 3rd edn, CEM, 2000). Nevertheless the Catholic Church accepts that in some situations, where all hope of recovery has gone, death should be allowed to occur naturally.

The hospice movement

Patients who are suffering from an incurable illness can be cared for in a hospice. Cicely Saunders, who started the movement, totally rejects euthanasia because she believes that terminally ill people can have a good quality of life if their pain is controlled and they receive emotional and spiritual support.

The Church of England says, 'The hospice movement is commended as a positive alternative, enabling people to be helped to die with dignity.

Figure G *Dame Cicely Saunders, a Christian, founded the first modern hospice in 1967. She said, 'I felt God was tapping me on the shoulder and telling me to get on with the work. I then started to plan the hospice and to raise money in the City. I never gave up hope, I knew it would happen.' How do you think the hospice movement might help people today?*

This work has enriched not only the lives of the terminally ill, but also those around them' (*What the Churches say on moral and social issues*, 3rd edn, CEM, 2000).

ACTIVITIES

2. Arrange the arguments about euthanasia into those that are completely against it and those who could accept some forms of euthanasia. Against each argument put the reason a Christian might give to support it.

3. Read each of the teachings about the sanctity of life and decide what implication each might have for euthanasia.

FOR RESEARCH

Find out where your nearest hospice is by asking at your public library, and try to discover some information about when it was founded. How is it funded? Why might Christians raise money for the hospice?

2 Christian attitudes to contraception and abortion

AIM

To understand the different attitudes among Christians to abortion and contraception and the reasons for them.

KEY TERM

contraception   preventing conception from ocurring

Christians believe that sexual love between a husband and wife is a gift from God that allows a married couple to express their love for each other fully and enables them to take their part in God's act of creation. Christians differ in the extent to which they believe they can intervene and take responsibility for preventing conception.

Figure H *Not all Christians agree that artificial forms of contraception should be used within a marriage. Why do some Christians believe using contraception is wrong?*

Christians who accept the use of **contraception** in marriage argue that there is nothing written in the Bible forbidding it. Jesus taught that love is what matters. Restricting the number of children to what a couple want and feel they can afford to support may be the most loving thing to do for every member of the family. Contraception can also prevent a woman's health suffering from a large number of pregnancies.

What the Churches say

The Anglican Church

The Church of England regards sexual love as an expression of a married couple's love for each other which strengthens their relationship. The Anglican Church accepts the use of all forms of contraception in that relationship because it allows a couple to enjoy sexual love but choose the best timing for, and size of, their family.

The Roman Catholic Church

Roman Catholics teach that the reason for a married couple having sex is to express their love for each other and take part in God's creative process by having children. The Catholic Church does not accept the use of contraception because it would prevent the act of sexual love being open to new life. If a married couple feel they must plan the number of children they have, then a 'natural family planning' method is advised.

Natural family planning, sometimes called the rhythm method, involves working out the days in a woman's menstrual cycle when she is least likely to conceive, then restricting lovemaking to those days.

The Catholic teachings on contraception were first given in the 1930s and reaffirmed by later Popes, most recently Pope John Paul II in his Humanae Vitae.

The reasons given by the Catholic Church are that:

- a couple promise in the marriage ceremony to have sex to have children, so using contraception would break that promise
- God commanded humans to go forth and multiply; using contraception disobeys this
- contraception encourages promiscuity which can lead to the spread of diseases such as HIV and AIDS
- contraception is unnatural and humans should accept what God gives.

The Salvation Army

Members of The Salvation Army believe that marriage is both a spiritual and a sexual union between husband and wife. They accept that couples may want to limit the number of children they have and that contraception is an acceptable way to do this.

Christian attitudes to abortion

Early in 2005 the Reverend Joanna Jepson took two doctors to court for performing an abortion at 28 weeks because the foetus had a cleft palate. The vicar herself had been born with similar problems which had been corrected by surgery. Although she lost the case on a legal point, Christians shared her concern about abortion. When a non-Christian suggested that the British government should lower the permitted time for abortion from 24 weeks to 20 weeks, British Christians united behind him.

Roman Catholics, and some evangelical Christians, believe that life begins at conception so abortion is murder. They argue that Christian teachings about the sanctity of life mean every human has the right to life (even a foetus) and abortion is a serious sin. Cardinal Cormac Murphy-O'Connor, Britain's most senior Catholic said, 'Abortion for Catholics is a very key issue – we are totally opposed to it.'

In 2005 the Archbishop of Canterbury said that with 500 abortions a day in England, 'People are realising we can't go on as we are…For a large majority of Christians…. it is impossible to regard abortion as anything other than the deliberate termination of a human life.' Recent developments in medical science led him to think abortion after 20 weeks was wrong because:

- a foetus can feel pain
- a foetus does have a level consciousness
- a foetus must have human rights of some kind
- medical science can save premature babies.

Whilst disliking abortion, some Christians accept that in certain circumstances abortion may be the kindest and most loving action – a mother's health might be at risk, the baby might be handicapped, the family could be too poor to look after another child or the pregnancy might be the result of rape. Christians who argue along these lines refer to Jesus' teaching that love is the most important thing.

ACTIVITIES

1. Read these two extracts from the Roman Catholic Catechism and write down what each teaches about contraception.
Called to give life, spouses share in the creative power and fatherhood of God. Married couples should regard it as their proper mission to transmit human life. Every action which proposes, whether as an end or as a means, to render procreation impossible is intrinsically evil.

2. Read what the Baptist Union says on these issues. What is their attitude towards abortion and contraception? What reasons are given?
Few[Baptists] absolutely reject abortion in all circumstances, recognising that in a fallen world it may be the lesser of two evils. Far better to prevent the conditions which lead to the necessity of abortion. (What the Churches say on moral and social issues, 3rd edn, CEM, 2000*).*

ACTIVITIES

1. Why do Christians think life is sacred? How could this affect their views on abortion or euthanasia?

2. Make a list of the non-religious arguments in favour of euthanasia and the non-religious arguments against it.

FOR RESEARCH

Parents of conjoined twins can be faced with difficult decisions involving the issue of the sanctity of life. How did the religious beliefs of the parents of conjoined twins Jodie and Mary influence their decisions? Visit www.heinemann.co.uk/hotlinks, type in the express code 2280P and click on this section to read more about this case.

Tackling an exam question

Here is a **(d)** question from the exam paper.

'Every woman should have the right to an abortion if she wants one.'
Do you agree? Give reasons for your opinion, showing you have considered another point of view. In your answer you should refer to Christianity. **(4)**

(Edexcel Unit B, 2004)

The question starts with a statement and the examiner wants you to show that you understand that person's point of view. You need to show that you also understand the opposite side of the argument. You are asked what *you* think so you should explain this in your conclusion. Do not forget that this answer must explain the different views Christians hold on this issue. More detailed help with answering a **(d)** question appears on page 123 along with the marking grid for this type of question.

Planning your answer to this question

1. Copy the question into your book and highlight or underline the important words.
2. When you are planning your answer, draw two columns for the different sides of the argument. Check you have put religious evidence into at least one column.
3. Decide what you will say to conclude.

Student's answer

Some people say a woman should be allowed to have an abortion because it is her body after all. She should be able to choose what she wants to do with it. Nobody has the right to tell her what to do. Another reason that she should be allowed to have an abortion is because having a baby might make her ill or even kill her. ✓ (Level 1)

People who disagree with abortions would say a baby is a gift from God. That means it can only be God's decision to take that life away. So they would be against abortion because of their religion.

I think a woman should be allowed to have an abortion. After all it is her life, she has got to carry the baby for nine months and she knows what is best for herself and the baby. ✓ (Level 2)

Examiner's comments

Religion is mentioned, but the candidate has not said which religion. Personal opinion is given. This is a Level 2 answer because it is a basic 'for and against' argument. The candidate did not do as the question asked, however, which was to 'refer to Christianity', so she can only get as far as Level 2. If the student had written, 'Some Christians argue that life begins at conception and so abortion is wrong because it is taking a life', then the answer could have gained Level 3. To get to Level 4 the candidate needed to develop both sides of the argument more fully and use them to reach her own conclusion.

Student's improved answer

Some people say a woman should be allowed to have an abortion because it is her body and she should be able to choose what she wants to do with it. She has free will; nobody has the right to tell her what to do with her own body. Another reason why she should be allowed to have an abortion is because having a baby might make her ill or even kill her. ✓ (L1)

People who disagree with abortion might say a baby is a gift from God. That means only God can decide to take its life away. Some Christians are against abortion because they believe in the sanctity of life and they think abortion is a sin. ✓ (L2) Some Christians argue life begins at conception so abortion is wrong. Abortion is taking a life and that is forbidden in the Ten Commandments. However, there are Christians who say that the life of the mother must take priority over that of her unborn child and abortion would be permitted if the mother's life were at risk. ✓ (L3)

I think a woman should be allowed to have an abortion under certain circumstances. After all it is her body and she is the one who has to carry the baby for nine months. I do not think it is fair if a girl who has been raped has to go through with an unwanted pregnancy. She would also be reminded of her attacker every time she saw the child. It would ruin her life and it would be a terrible life for a child who was not loved or wanted. ✓ (L4)

Level 1 (1 mark)

For a point of view supported by one relevant reason.

Level 2 (2 marks)

For a basic for and against, or a reasoned opinion, or well argued points of view with no personal opinion.

Level 3 (3 marks)

For a reasoned personal opinion, using religious/moral argument, referring to another point of view.

Level 4 (4 marks)

For a coherent, reasoned personal opinion, using religious/moral argument, evaluating another point of view to reach a personal conclusion.

3 a) Definition required here (see p. 24).

b) Be clear which group you are talking about. Name them and say what their views are. Try to cover all the views you have learned. Pages 36–7 will help you.

c) Remember to say *what* the attitudes are and *why* people believe what they do. Look at pages 28–9 for help.

d) This is your chance to give a personal opinion. Say *what* you think and *why*. Then state what people who disagree with you say and why. Pages 30–1 deal with this issue. Remember to give a Christian view (see pp. 36–7). Sum up with your conclusion. Page 123 will help you answer this type of question.

Questions 3(b), 3(c) and 4(b) are taken from Edexcel Unit B paper 2004.

SECTION TWO: MATTERS OF LIFE AND DEATH

You must answer ONE question from this section.

EITHER QUESTION 3

3 a) What does *paranormal* mean? **(2)**

b) Outline different attitudes to contraception in Christianity. **(6)**

c) Explain why there are different attitudes about what happens after death in Christianity. **(8)**

d) *'Abortion is never the right solution.'*
Do you agree? Give reasons for your opinion, showing you have considered another point of view. In your answer you should refer to at least one religion. **(4)**

(Total 20 marks)

Leave blank

Q3

OR QUESTION 4

4 a) What does *abortion* mean? **(2)**

b) Outline British law on abortion. **(6)**

c) Explain why there are different attitudes towards euthanasia in Christianity. **(8)**

d) *'Near-death experiences are proof of life after death.'*
Do you agree? Give reasons for your opinion, showing that you have considered another point of view. In your answer, you should refer to Christianity. **(4)**

(Total 20 marks)

Q4

---

4 a) Keep your definition brief (see p. 30).

b) Remember, it does say 'outline' so don't get carried away with lots of detail.

c) You need to state *what* the different Christian attitudes are and, for each one, *why* they believe it. Pages 34–5 will help you with the points, page 122 gives help on writing a **(c)** answer.

d) Your views are requested so you could begin, 'I think... because... '. Then give a different viewpoint. Make sure you have included what a Christian would say about near-death experiences. Consult pages 24–9 and page 123 for help with writing a **(d)** answer. Make sure you conclude with what you think, and why.

Figure A A traditional family group.

Figure B A single mother with two children from different relationships.

In this chapter you will learn:

- about the changing attitudes in the UK to cohabitation and marriage
- about the purposes of marriage in Christianity, including the main features of a Christian marriage ceremony (faithfulness)
- about differences among Christians in their attitudes to sex outside marriage (pre-marital sex, promiscuity and adultery) including the reasons for these attitudes
- about changing attitudes to divorce in the UK
- about differences among Christians in their attitudes to divorce (including annulment and re-marriage) including the reasons for these attitudes
- about the changing nature of family life (nuclear family, extended family, re-constituted family) in the UK
- about the teachings of Christianity on family life and its importance
- how churches help with the upbringing of children and keeping the family together
- about changing attitudes to homosexuality in the UK
- about Christian attitudes to homosexuality and the reasons for these attitudes.

The key terms you must know are:

cohabitation, marriage, faithfulness, pre-marital sex, promiscuity, adultery, annulment, re-marriage, nuclear family, extended family, re-constituted family, homosexuality

ACTIVITIES

1. Study Figures A and B with a partner. Figure A shows a typical family group in the 1950s. Figure B shows a modern-day family group. What do these photographs show you about changes in attitudes towards relationships and family life?

2. As a class, list the advantages and disadvantages of each type of family.

AIM

To understand changing attitudes in the UK towards sexual relationships outside marriage.

KEY TERMS

adultery an act of sexual intercourse between a married person and someone other than their marriage partner

cohabitation living together without being married

faithfulness staying with your marriage partner and having sex only with them

marriage the condition of a man and woman legally united for the purpose of living together and, usually, having children

pre-marital sex sex before marriage

promiscuity having sex with a number of partners without commitment

GOALIE CAUGHT 'PLAYING AWAY'

Celebs divorce imminent

'I won't have her back at any price,' says duped husband

DNA test for love rat

'I'll bring my baby up alone,' says top executive

British attitudes towards sexual relationships

If newspapers are anything to go by, the virtue we prize most is **faithfulness**. The celebrity who 'cheats' on his partner is the one who comes in for the most condemnation. For many people it does not matter whether a couple are married to each other or not, what matters is whether trust has been betrayed. If a couple are married and one of them has a sexual affair with somebody outside of the marriage, it is called **adultery**.

There has been a big change in British attitudes towards sexual relationships. In the past couples who had **pre-marital sex** were thought to be immoral and those who cohabited were said to be 'living in sin'. Sex outside of marriage was considered wrong because, since contraception was hard to obtain, there was a high chance a woman would become pregnant and her child would not be born into the traditional family structure. If a couple have sex before they are married it is called pre-marital sex. This might be a one-night stand or part of a more meaningful relationship.

Cohabitation

Today many couples live together before marrying. This enables them to find out whether they are suited. If they are not, they can split up and avoid a divorce. **Cohabitation** involves setting up home together and enjoying a sexual relationship in the same way as a married couple. The big difference is that there is no legal commitment to each other, although a cohabiting couple may have commitments such as a mortgage or even children.

In English law, cohabiting relationships are recognised as 'common law' marriages, but cohabiting couples have fewer rights than married ones. Some cohabiting couples might choose to marry later if they want to have children. Others see no reason for a legal or religious commitment and continue to cohabit happily for the rest of their lives.

ACTIVITIES

1. List the advantages and disadvantages of cohabitation.

2. Why do you think some people decide to get married when they want to have children?

○ For discussion

If someone has casual sex with various partners without commitment or love, it is called **promiscuity**. Most people think promiscuity is a bad thing. Why is that?

ACTIVITIES

3. What is the difference between promiscuity and adultery?

4. Why do you think many people say promiscuity is bad but cohabitation is good?

Criticism of cohabitation

Statistically, unmarried couples who live together are more likely to split up than married couples. Critics also say that living together without proper commitment encourages a casual attitude to the relationship so that neither partner will bother to show much care or consideration to the other. Cohabiting couples might think that if they get bored with their partner, they can move in with someone else. Some people believe that it is not necessary for couples to live together to find out if they are compatible or not. Couples who have lived together and then marry, still get divorced, so it does not guarantee anything.

The Salvation Army 'is aware that many today choose to live together, as though husband and wife, without marriage'. However, it believes that such a relationship still falls short of God's ideal will.

This, as revealed in scripture, is for sexual union to be expressed in the context of marriage. Resulting children can then be nurtured in the knowledge that their biological parents, or adoptive parents if this is the case, are mutually committed to this way. The emotional, psychological and physical security flowing from this is likely to afford the most helpful environment for their upbringing. (*What the Churches say on moral and social issues*, 3rd edn, CEM, 2000)

Marriage is still very popular

Despite the changing attitude towards sex outside **marriage**, many people still get married. It is not just religious people who choose marriage because there are just as many civil weddings today. Some people even return to get married again after their previous marriage has ended. That suggests marriage has something which cohabitation does not.

FOR RESEARCH

Find out more about the legal rights a couple have if they cohabit. How are these different to the rights a married couple have? A good area to look at is the rights married and unmarried couples have in relation to their children.

Divorce

Unfortunately, changing attitudes mean that divorce is more common. It is estimated that one in three marriages now end in divorce. Most people understand that things can go wrong and they think it might be better for all concerned if a couple separate and begin a new life.

○ For discussion

As a class, discuss what you think of the idea that 'Marriage should not be for life. Couples should take out a contract for five or ten years with an option on renewal'.

ACTIVITIES

5. Why do you think that the Salvation Army is against cohabitation?

6. Which group of Christians do you think shares the same views as the Salvation Army (see page 36)?

7. Why do you think people still want to get married today even though one in three marriages end in divorce?

Christian attitudes towards sexual relationships

AIM

To understand differences among Christians in their attitudes to sex outside marriage and the reasons for these attitudes.

KEY TERMS

adultery an act of sexual intercourse between a married person and someone other than their marriage partner
pre-marital sex sex before marriage
promiscuity having sex with a number of partners without commitment

STARTER

With a partner work out two arguments in favour of pre-marital sex and two arguments against it.

For Christians sex is an act of love and of commitment that should take place within marriage. This is not just because marriage is a traditional Christian relationship between a man and a woman, but because many Christians believe restricting sex to marriage is in the best interests of society, children and the individual.

While sex within marriage is the ideal for all Christians, there is a difference of opinion among Christian groups in their attitude towards sex outside of marriage.

What do the Churches say?

- The attitude of the Roman Catholic Church towards sexual relationship outside marriage is clearly stated in the Catechism of the Catholic Church: 'The sexual act must take place exclusively within marriage. Outside marriage it always constitutes a grave sin'. Pre-marital sex as well as adultery is forbidden, so cohabitation is not an option for a Roman Catholic couple considering marriage.

Figure C *These teenagers are members of Silver Ring Thing, an organisation which disagrees with pre-marital sex. Visit their website at www.heinemann.co.uk/hotlinks to find out more. Type in the express code 2280P and click on this section to access their website.*

Other Christian denominations, such as the Methodists, believe that sex belongs within marriage because there are many Biblical teachings to support this.

The Ten Commandments state, 'You shall not commit adultery'. (Exodus 20: 14)

Jesus added, 'I tell you, anyone who looks at a woman and wants to possess her is guilty of committing adultery with her in his heart'. (Matthew 19: 9)

St Paul warned early Christians, 'Avoid immorality. Any other sin a man commits does not affect his body; but the man who is guilty of sexual immorality sins against his own body. Do you not know that your body is the temple of the Holy Spirit who lives in you and who was given to you by God'. (1 Corinthians 6: 18–19)

- Some Protestant groups, although preferring sex to exist exclusively in a married relationship, understand times have changed. These Christians are prepared to accept cohabitation if it is a prelude to marriage.
- The General Synod of the Church of England recognised that family life in Britain has changed and expressed regret that many couples were now choosing to cohabit. However, in their report 'Something to Celebrate' (1995), the Church agreed to welcome cohabiting couples in the church and encourage them to regard cohabitation as a prelude to Christian marriage.
- Some liberal Christian groups, such as Quakers, accept that sex does take place outside marriage. Their main concern is whether pre-marital sex causes harm or good to the people involved in the relationship.

Sexual activity is essentially neither good nor evil; it is a normal biological activity, which like most other human activities can be indulged in destructively or creatively. (Quaker Faith & Practice, 22: 13)

Human sexuality is a divine gift, forming part of the complex union of body, mind and spirit which is our humanity. The sexual expression of a loving relationship can bring delight, joy and faithfulness. (Quaker Faith & Practice, 22: 11)

Adultery and promiscuity

Adultery, however, remains totally unacceptable to all Christians because it breaks the vow of faithfulness made in the presence of God at the marriage ceremony. Also Christians believe adultery is wrong because it involves deceit and people can get hurt. Promiscuity is unacceptable to all Christians because it is an action undertaken without care or regard for other people. For many Christians, promiscuity is a misuse of God's gift of sexual love.

PATH TO THE TOP

Roman Catholic priests are not permitted to marry or have any sexual relationships. Priests in the Protestant Church are encouraged to marry and have families. A **celibate** is a person who chooses not to marry or have sex. A few Christians choose celibacy, as Jesus did, because it enables them to concentrate on worshipping God without the distractions of family life. Read what St Paul says about celibacy in 1 Corinthians 7: 32–5.

ACTIVITIES

1. 'Restricting sex to marriage is best for society, for children and for the individual.' List the reasons why the categories mentioned might benefit from sex being restricted to marriage. Then list reasons against this argument.

2. Create a fact file on different Christian attitudes towards pre-marital sex using the material on these pages. Make sure you include the reasons why these groups hold the views they do.

AIM

To understand changing attitudes towards homosexuality in the UK and to understand why there are differences among Christians in their attitudes towards homosexuality.

KEY TERM

homosexuality   sexual attraction to people of the same gender

Changing attitudes

Through the ages, and in all societies, there have been some people who are sexually attracted to people of the same gender as themselves. This is called **homosexuality**. In the past in Britain any sexual act between men was a criminal offence and homosexuals were sent to prison for their actions. Sexual relations between two women were never mentioned in the law, so lesbian activities have never been illegal.

In 1967, this law changed to allow sex in private between consenting men over the age of 21. In 1994, the age was lowered to 18. After further pressure from the gay community to treat homosexuals and heterosexuals (that is people who have sex with people of the opposite gender) equally, the age of consent was lowered to 16 in 1998.

Although homosexuality between men or women over the age of 16 is now legal, this group of people still find themselves discriminated against. Homosexual partners are not permitted to marry and same-sex couples find it difficult to adopt a child. If their partner dies, the survivor in a homosexual relationship does not have the same automatic rights of inheritance as a widow or widower. Homosexuals have also found themselves the victims of harassment and attacks.

Figure D *In 2003 there was a heated debate in the Anglican Church about homosexuality when the Reverend Dr Jeffrey John was named bishop of Reading. He made no secret of his long-term celibate homosexual relationship and campaigned for gay rights. Parts of the Anglican Church were convinced that this was wrong. What arguments could they use to support their case? Is it right that Dr John was forced to stand down?*

Christian attitudes towards homosexuality

The Bible forbids same-sex relationships. The Old Testament says, 'No man is to have sexual relations with another man; God hates that'. (Leviticus 18: 22)

The New Testament says, 'Even the women pervert the natural use of their sex by unnatural acts. In the same way the men give up natural sexual relations with women and burn with passion for each other. Men do shameful things with each other, and as a result they bring upon themselves the punishment they deserve for their wrongdoing'. (Romans 1: 26–8)

However, there is a difference of opinion between Christian groups, and sometimes even within the same church, about homosexuality. The New Testament words above were written by St Paul; Jesus himself never spoke about homosexuality, but he did support married relationships between men and women.

Most Christians today accept that a person does not choose to be homosexual; it is an inclination they are born with. For this reason it would be unfair to condemn someone for his or her natural tendency. However, the majority of Christians make a distinction between inclination and sexual practice.

- Many evangelical Christians, who follow the teachings of the Bible and those of the early Church closely, believe the tendency towards and practice of homosexuality is sinful.
- Roman Catholics accept some Christians may have an inclination to be homosexual. In that case they should lead a celibate life (one without sex). Because the Roman Catholic Church believes that sexual activity can only take place between a married couple, homosexual activity is therefore automatically ruled out. Equally, because the sex act must be open to God's gift of a baby, homosexual sex is unacceptable. Catholics look to the Bible, traditions of the Church and Papal teachings to support this view.

- The Church of England is divided over the issue of homosexuality. They accept that some members of the Church may be practising homosexuals, indeed there is a Gay Christian Movement, but not all Anglicans believe this is right. The issue of ordaining practising homosexuals as bishops almost split the Church in 2003 and, after much heart-searching, was rejected. Anglicans believe the Bible condemns homosexual activity, but they point to accounts of close same-sex friendships in the Bible, such as those of David and Jonathan and Ruth and Naomi, which are accepted and admired.

The Church of England produced the following statement after much difficult discussion about homosexuality, 'If we are faithful to Our Lord, then disagreement over the proper expression of homosexual love will never become rejection of the homosexual person.'

- Some liberal Christians, such as Quakers, accept that homosexual relationships can be stable, loving, long-term relationships. Quakers welcome gay people into membership in the same way as heterosexuals, because they believe religion is a spiritual issue not a sexual one. Most Quakers would argue that the Bible reflects the attitudes of the time and society in which it was written, so some passages may not be appropriate for the twenty-first century. Jesus taught that love was what mattered most.

ACTIVITIES

1. Why are Christians divided over the issue of homosexuality?

2. Draw a chart with four columns, one for each of the views stated here. Write what each group believes in your chart, along with the reasons.

For discussion

If Christians practised what they preached, they would accept everybody. Discuss this issue as a class.

AIM

To understand the purpose of Christian marriage including the main features of the marriage ceremony.

KEY TERM

faithfulness staying with your marriage partner and having sex only with them

STARTER

Look carefully at Figure E and note down all the things you can see that you associate with a traditional Christian wedding ceremony. Add any other features which do not appear in the picture but which you think are an essential part of the ceremony. Which features have religious significance and which are simply traditional?

The purpose of Christian marriage

Christians believe marriage is the ideal way for a man and woman to live together in a lifelong relationship. The Bible says, 'For this reason a man will leave his father and mother and unite with his wife, and the two will become one'. (Mark 10: 7–8)

Marriage is a sacred union blessed by God and some Christians believe it can only end with the death of a partner. Faithfulness is part of Christian marriage and the couple promise this in their vows to each other.

Christians do not believe it is essential that they marry. People can remain single as Jesus did, but they should not enter into a sexual relationship with anyone. Marriage, however, is encouraged and particularly marriage to another Christian because it is hoped the couple will have children who will be brought up in the Christian faith.

PATH TO THE TOP

A popular reading at a Christian marriage ceremony is 1 Corinthians 13. Why do you think this passage is read at this time? List the virtues that St Paul says love should have.

The Anglican approach to marriage

Read what the Anglican Church says about the purpose of marriage:

It is God's purpose that a husband and wife give themselves to each other in love throughout their lives, they shall be united in that love as Christ is united with his Church. Marriage is given, that husband and wife may comfort and help each other, living faithfully together in need and in plenty, in sorrow and in joy. It is given, that with delight and tenderness, they may know each other in love, and through the joy of their bodily union, may strengthen the unions of their hearts and lives.

Figure E *What can you see in this image that you associate with a traditional wedding ceremony?*

It is given, that they may have children and be blessed in caring for them, and bringing them up in accordance with God's will, to his praise and glory. (*The Alternative Service Book 1980*, SPCK, p. 288)

The Roman Catholic approach to marriage

During a Roman Catholic wedding ceremony the following is said:

Father you have made the bond of marriage a holy mystery, a symbol of Christ's love for his Church… In the love of man and wife, God shows us a wonderful reflection of his own eternal love. (Geddes & Griffiths, *Christian Belief and Practice: The Roman Catholic Tradition*, Heinemann, 2002)

The couple are also asked, 'Are you ready to accept children lovingly from God, and bring them up according to the law of Christ and his Church?' (Geddes & Griffiths, *Christian Belief and Practice: The Roman Catholic Tradition*, Heinemann, 2002)

Other approaches to marriage

Other Christians would add that any marriage is a legal contract that protects the rights of each partner and any children born to them. Children of that marriage are recognised as 'legitimate', which gives them rights of inheritance. For some people, marriage is also important because it unites two families.

Key features of a Christian marriage ceremony

- The ceremony takes place in a church in the presence of God who is part of the marriage. Members of the congregation are human witnesses. 'I call upon these persons here present to witness that I [Name] do take you [Name] to be my lawful wedded husband/wife.'
- The couple make vows to each other, with God as their witness. 'I [Name] take you [Name] to be my husband/wife. To have and to hold from this day forward; for better, for worse, for richer, for poorer, in sickness and in health, to love and to cherish, till death us do part, according to God's holy law; and this is my solemn vow.'
- The Bible readings and the priest's talk are about Christian marriage.
- There are prayers to ask for God's blessing.
- There is the giving of a ring to symbolise the unending nature of love and the marriage. 'I give you this ring as a sign of our marriage. With my body I honour you, all that I am I give to you, and all that I have I share with you, within the love of God, Father, Son and Holy Spirit.' (*The Alternative Service Book 1980*, SPCK, p. 292)

ACTIVITIES

1. List the different points made by the Anglican Church regarding the purpose of marriage. Do you think a cohabiting couple could also achieve this? Why?

2. List the additional points that a Roman Catholic marriage ceremony makes about the purpose of marriage.

3. Copy the grid below and fill in the columns using information on these pages. Include anything else you know or can find out about Christian marriage. Check that each feature you have listed has a religious significance for Christians – bridesmaids, confetti and wedding cake are traditional features, but are not religious.

Main features of the Christian marriage ceremony	Significance and meaning of these features

3 Christian attitudes to the break up of a marriage

AIM

To understand differences among Christians in their attitudes to divorce, annulment and re-marriage and the reasons for these attitudes.

STARTER

As a class, discuss this statement: 'A couple are less likely to divorce if they have had a Christian marriage'. Do you agree with that? Why?

KEY TERMS

annulment a declaration by the Church that a marriage never lawfully existed

re-marriage marrying again after being divorced from a previous marriage

Divorce today

Attitudes towards divorce have changed a great deal in the last 50 years. In the past, divorce was uncommon because it was difficult and expensive to obtain. It was also frowned upon and divorcees frequently found themselves shunned by society as though they had been immoral.

Since that time there have been changes in the law to make it easier for people to end marriages that have failed; today one in three marriages ends in divorce. The most common grounds for a divorce are that the marriage has 'irretrievably broken down' perhaps because of adultery, desertion or cruelty. Because divorce is more common today, it is also more acceptable.

Christianity and divorce

Jesus said, 'A man will leave his father and mother and unite with his wife and the two will become one. So they are no longer two, but one. Man must not separate, then, what God has joined together… A man who divorces his wife and marries another woman commits adultery against his wife. In the same way, a woman who divorces her husband and marries another man commits adultery'. (Mark 10: 7–9, 11–12)

Jesus also said, 'I tell you then that any man who divorces his wife for any cause other than her unfaithfulness, commits adultery if he marries some other woman.' (Matthew 19: 9)

Christians recognise that not all marriages work and that some people will want to end their marriages. However, Christians differ in their attitudes towards divorce.

Figure F Christians accept that there will be times when couples fall out. They are human after all, but every effort should be made to sort out their differences and forgive each other.

Christian marriage is a legal contract as well as a religious one so all divorces have to go through a court of law. There is, nonetheless, a religious aspect because the vows are made in church before God and most Christians do not like the idea of breaking sacred promises.

The Roman Catholic view

The Roman Catholic Church does not accept divorce in any form because vows taken for life cannot be broken. If a marriage has broken down, the couple can live apart but they must remain celibate and never enter into a sexual relationship with anyone else. That would be adultery.

In a few cases Roman Catholics are permitted to have an **annulment**. This means a marriage is invalid and never truly existed. Annulments are not common and the Catholic Marriage Tribunal will only permit an annulment if they are convinced that:

- the marriage was not made freely i.e. an arranged marriage
- one of the partners did not have a full understanding of what they were doing i.e. they were not of sound mind
- the marriage was not lawful i.e. if one of the partners was already married.

Orthodox and liberal view

Some Orthodox Christians and liberal Protestants will permit divorce if it is the lesser of two evils, but it is strongly discouraged. They agree that, in some cases, more hurt could be caused to the family (which might include children) if a failed marriage is forced to continue. Because Jesus taught his followers that love was the most important thing, permitting divorce might be the most loving thing to do in some cases.

For discussion

'Everybody makes mistakes and so divorce should be allowed once'. Do you agree? What would a Christian say to this?

FOR RESEARCH

To understand the change that has occurred in attitudes to divorce, find out what happened to Edward VIII, the British monarch, in 1936 when he wanted to marry a divorcee.

Re-marriage

Since the Roman Catholic Church does not permit divorce, it cannot consider **re-marriage** for divorcees. If a person has lost their spouse through death, then re-marriage in the Catholic Church is permitted.

Some Christians who accept divorce will not permit another religious marriage ceremony in church. They argue that if sacred vows have been broken, the same vows cannot be taken again. Other Christians, such as members of the Baptist Union and the Church of England, permit re-marriage in church because they believe God will forgive sins and allow people to make a fresh start. The issue of re-marriage in church is still much debated by Christians. Some priests do not believe it is right to conduct a marriage ceremony for divorcees who have broken their previous vows. Most churches do permit these priests to refuse to conduct the ceremony provided they allow another minister, sympathetic to re-marriage, to take the ceremony instead.

ACTIVITIES

1. Which of the Bible passages would a Protestant use to show that Jesus did permit divorce in some circumstances?

2. What evidence is contained in the Bible passages that could be used by the Roman Catholic Church to show Jesus disapproved of divorce?

3. Explain the difference between annulment and divorce.

KEY TERMS

extended family children, parents and grandparents/aunts/uncles living as a unit or in close proximity

nuclear family mother, father and children living as a unit

re-constituted family where two sets of children (step-brothers and sisters) become one family when their divorced parents marry each other

STARTER

With a partner, work out what you think is the relationship between the people in Figure G. Compare this picture with Figures A and B on page 41. What has caused these changes in family life?

Re-constituted families

Some divorced couples who re-marry bring with them children from a previous marriage to form a new family. This is called a **re-constituted family**. It is likely to mean that there are step-brothers and step-sisters in the new family.

Changing families

New developments in family groupings include single-parent families, possibly formed following a family break-up, and re-constituted families which are created when a couple re-marry and bring children from their former marriages to the new family.

It is likely that the young woman in Figure B (page 41) is a single parent bringing up her children on her own. A **nuclear family** is where a father and mother are living together with their children.

In previous centuries it was quite usual to find several generations of a family either living together or living close by as an **extended family**. In the days before the National Health Service and state benefits, families had to look after relatives who were sick or elderly. Living nearby made this easier. Grandparents often played their part by helping with childcare and sharing with the family living expenses. Anyone in the family who went through a difficult time, emotionally or financially, could rely on their relatives to help them through. Today extended families are less common.

ACTIVITIES

1. Make a list of possible reasons for the rise in single-parent families in recent years. Pages 42–5 might help you. Do not forget to consider religious as well as non-religious people.

2. Against each type of family group, list the advantages and disadvantages you think might arise from belonging to it.

Figure G How do you think the people in this photo are related?

Figure H This is one of the Ten Commandments so Christians take this commandment about family life seriously. What could a family do to carry it out?

Christianity and family life

Christians believe the family was created by God as the best environment in which a couple can live and raise children. The Old Testament has many references to the importance of family life and the Gospels show Jesus was a member of a family, cared for by his mother and father; indeed there are references to Jesus having brothers and sisters. For Christians this is proof that the family is a God-given unit and the Church's teachings support this.

Having children is one of the purposes of Christian marriage. Parents are encouraged to bring up their children in a loving home where they will be taught right from wrong and learn about Christian values and the Christian lifestyle. Not only do children benefit from this arrangement, but people believe that family units help maintain a stable society because everyone knows how to behave.

Children are not the only ones to benefit from family life. Everyone, from the youngest to the oldest, receives life's basic necessities such as food and shelter, as well as love, emotional support and comfort from other family members.

What the Churches say

The Salvation Army

The Salvation Army believes that family life, based on marriage, 'is the bedrock of a stable society and wishes to do all it can to promote families and marriage … It recognises that the sense of belonging which begins with family can lead to a sense of belonging to the community and ultimately to an awareness of belonging to God.' (*What the Churches say on moral and social issues*, 3rd edn, CEM, 2000)

The Baptist Union

The Baptist Union says that, 'For many people, their key relationships are those they have with members of their own families. These families may be of many different kinds and sizes: extended families, households, small communities sharing accommodation. The Bible should not be understood to endorse only the nuclear family. In fact the Old Testament demonstrates that God has a special concern for lone parents and children without fathers. Families of every kind offer the possibility of life in community, of life in relationship with others; it is this that is important, not any one particular model of the family'. (*What the Churches say on moral and social issues*, 3rd edn, CEM, 2000)

The Roman Catholic Church

Roman Catholics say that, 'One of the main responsibilities of married couples is to provide an atmosphere of goodness in the home. They are also bound to raise their children with Christian values… It has been proven that no matter how much outside instruction children receive, it will avail nothing if values are not carried out in the home. The nurturing of the children in the faith is one of the most serious responsibilities parents have'. (*The Essential Catholic Handbook*, Canterbury Press, 1997)

ACTIVITIES

3. What does The Salvation Army say is the advantage of Christian family life? What is their reasoning?

4. What are the Baptist Union's views on different family groups?

MARRIAGE AND THE FAMILY

KEY TERM

faithfulness staying with your marriage partner and having sex only with them

From cradle to grave

The Christian Church provides guidance and support for every member of the family throughout their life. That is because Jesus taught his followers to love one another and treat others as they would like to be treated themselves.

Welcoming a child into the Christian family

Many Christian groups welcome a baby into their community soon after birth with a ceremony of baptism or dedication (see pages 10–11). Along with the godparents and parents, the congregation promises to teach the child about their religion and to encourage him or her to be confirmed when they are old enough. Baptism services frequently take place during morning worship to show that the child is part of this congregation of Christians. Everyone has their part to play in helping that child to grow up in the Christian faith and supporting the child throughout his or her life.

Growing up as a Christian

Parents do not just *teach* their children about Christianity they also *show* them how to lead a good Christian life by their example.

- The family is likely to attend Sunday worship in church and worship at festivals such as Christmas and Easter.

- The children may well attend a Sunday School each week to receive further instruction in Christian beliefs.
- Many churches have a monthly family service where children can worship alongside their parents. Family services are usually shorter and take into account the needs and interests of the younger members of the community.
- At festivals such as Christmas, children learn more about their religion from gospel stories, nativity plays and carol singing.
- As children move into their teens, the Church may encourage them to consider being confirmed into membership of the Christian community. Special evening classes are run for people considering confirmation (see page 11).

Some churches run social clubs for children with a strong Christian ethos. The very youngest children might go to mother-and-toddler clubs and playgroups run by the church. Some churches run Brownies, Guides, Cubs, Scouts, or Boys' or Girls' Brigade and Christian youth clubs for teenagers.

Some parents choose a primary or secondary school run by the Church for their child's education. As well as studying National Curriculum subjects, pupils there are encouraged to follow the Christian lifestyle.

Helping adult Christians

Figure I *How do you think discussion groups like this might help Christians learn about Christianity?*

When a Christian couple is considering getting married and starting a family, the Church is on hand to advise them. People usually go to talk to their priest as part of their preparation for marriage. At a later stage they might join a social club run by the Church for young men or wives and mothers to help them keep a Christian home.

If things go wrong, the priest is on hand to discuss marital problems and some churches can offer counselling or marriage guidance. For families facing emotional difficulties or financial hardship, help can come from a Christian charity. This help might be specialist advice in the event of a family break-up or counselling and support at times of bereavement. Some Christian charities can offer financial support if illness or redundancy creates hardship for a family.

"... I was **hungry** and you gave me something to eat... I was a **stranger** and you invited me in... I was **sick** and you looked after me, I was in **prison** and you came to visit me."

Matthew 25: 35-36

Put your faith into action. Pray for, preach about and participate in our work with children at risk on the streets, young refugees, disabled children and children in trouble with the law.

For more information contact us today:
0845 300 1128
supporteraction@childrenssociety.org.uk
www.childrenssociety.org.uk

Photographs modelled for The Children's Society
Charity Registration No. 221124

The Children's Society

With children, for children, with you

Figure J *The Children's Society is a Christian charity that can assist families facing difficulties.*

Christian care of the elderly

Christians take the obligation to respect their parents seriously. Church groups often run special lunches and social clubs for older people. If elderly relatives can no longer care for themselves, and their family are not able to care for them in the home, there are residential homes for the elderly run by Christian organisations.

Here is what one Christian group says about the support they give to families.

The Salvation Army seeks to promote family life and to play whatever role it can in preventing its breakdown or demise… The Salvation Army is keenly aware and sensitively conscious of those many family units in which a parent is forced by circumstances to raise a family, for example following bereavement, divorce or legal separation. To these family units The Army offers support and care… The Salvation Army works widely with couples experiencing marital difficulties and with families under stress. It is realistic about the frailty of human nature and recognises that some marriages fail.
(What the Churches say on moral and social issues, 3rd edn, 2000)

ACTIVITIES

1. What support does The Salvation Army offer families? Why does it do that?

2. Draw an imaginary person's timeline 'from cradle to grave'. He or she can have various disasters befall them, which require assistance. At various points in their life, indicate how the Church could support them or their family.

3. Why might Christians choose to run an organisation like the Children's Society? Look at their website, or write to them (their address appears on page 136) to find out how their work helps to support the Christian idea of family life.

4. Prepare a presentation you could give to the class on the way churches support family life.

3 Putting it all together

For discussion

Does it make any difference where a marriage takes place? Does a religious setting create a more serious approach to marriage than a Las Vegas wedding?

ACTIVITIES

1. Write a paragraph explaining why Christians believe that a man and a woman should get married before they live together.

2. Outline the different Christian attitudes to homosexuality.

3. Divide your page into four sections.

- In section one, write down non-religious arguments in favour of cohabitation.
- In section two, write down non-religious arguments against sex before marriage.
- In section three, write down the different Christian attitudes towards sex before marriage.
- In section four, write down the different Christian attitudes towards divorce.

4. With a partner try to work out why some Christians refer to couples who cohabit as 'living in sin'?

Tackling an exam question

Here is a **(c)** question from the exam paper.

> <u>Explain</u> why there are <u>different attitudes</u> to <u>re-marriage</u> in <u>Christianity</u>. **(8)**
>
> *(Edexcel Unit A, 2004)*

Planning your answer to this question

1. Underline the important words in the question. (This has already been done for you in this instance.) You can see there are two parts to this question: firstly, *what* are the different attitudes and, secondly, *why* are there different attitudes? You will have to tackle both aspects if you want to reach the top grades.

2. The important thing to notice in this question is that it says re-marriage not divorce. They are slightly different so be careful!

3. Look back at pages 50–1 in this book if you need to refresh your memory. List the attitudes you are going to include. Write a reason for that attitude against each one. Try to include a specialist term in your answer if possible.

HINT

The **(c)** question carries more marks than any of the other parts of the paper. It is worth 8 marks. The examiner is trying to discover two things. *Do you know the facts* and *do you understand the reasons behind the facts*. The more detail you give, the better the level you will attain.

Student's answer

In Christianity there are different attitudes towards re-marriage. Roman Catholics say you should only get married once. And they mean once, because you aren't allowed to get divorced. The couple have made their vows before God and so they should do their best to remain married and so re-marrying is seen as wrong. ✓ (Level 1)

Protestants on the other hand, are not as concerned about failed marriages so long as both people have got a good reason for splitting up. They are allowed to re-marry so long as the previous marriage ended due to legitimate circumstances. ✓ (Level 2)

Examiner's comments

The student has reached Level 2, scoring 4 marks. They have given a basic answer that shows they do understand that there are two different Christian responses to re-marriage. However, they have not told the examiner the reasons for these different attitudes.

To attain Level 3, the student could have given more detail about the reasons why Protestants allow re-marriage. To reach Level 4, the student needed to show he really understood the differences in Christian attitudes to re-marriage.

Level 1 (2 marks)

For a simple, appropriate and relevant idea.

Level 2 (4 marks)

For a basic explanation showing understanding of a relevant idea.

Level 3 (6 marks)

For a developed explanation showing understanding of the main idea(s) using some specialist vocabulary.

Level 4 (8 marks)

For a comprehensive explanation showing a coherent understanding of the main idea(s) and using specialist language appropriately.

Student's improved answer

In Christianity there are different attitudes towards re-marriage. Roman Catholics say you should only get married once. And they mean once, because you aren't allowed to get divorced. The couple have made their vows before God and so they should do their best to remain married and so re-marrying is seen as wrong. ✓ (L1)

Protestants on the other hand, are not as concerned about failed marriages so long as both people have got a good reason for splitting up. They are allowed to re-marry so long as the previous marriage ended due to legitimate circumstances. ✓ (L2) Protestants allow re-marriage because they believe God forgives sins and lets people have a second chance. ✓ (L3)

Although many Protestant churches allow people to get divorced, however, some do not permit re-marriage in church. They say it is impossible to take the same vows again and say you will keep them for life if you have just broken them. ✓ (L4)

MARRIAGE AND THE FAMILY

5 **a)** Clear definition required (see p. 42).

b) The answer requires a concise account of the different views Christians hold on this subject. Pages 44–5 will help you.

c) Explain what Christian family life is like and how it is supported by the religion (see pp. 52–5). There are two bits to this answer! See page 122 for help with this sort of question.

d) Say what you think about divorce and why. Then say what other people think and why. One of those viewpoints should be clearly linked to Christianity (see pp. 50–1). Make sure you come to a conclusion and explain it. Page 123 will help you write this sort of evaluative answer.

Question 5(c) is based on a question from the Edexcel Unit B Specimen Paper. Question 6(a) is taken from Edexcel Unit B paper 2004. Question 6(c) is taken from Edexcel Unit B Specimen Paper.

SECTION THREE: MARRIAGE AND THE FAMILY

You must answer ONE question from this section.

EITHER QUESTION 5

5 **a)** What is *promiscuity*? **(2)**

b) Outline different Christian attitudes towards sex before marriage. **(6)**

c) Explain why family life is important for Christians. **(8)**

d) *'Divorce is bad for everybody.'*
Do you agree? Give reasons for your opinion, showing you have considered another point of view. In your answer you should refer to Christianity. **(4)**

(Total 20 marks)

OR QUESTION 6

6 **a)** What is an *extended family*? **(2)**

b) Describe how churches help families with the upbringing of children. **(6)**

c) Explain how a Christian wedding ceremony may help a marriage to succeed. **(8)**

d) *'Living together is less of a gamble than marriage.'*
Do you agree? Give reasons for your opinion, showing you have considered another point of view. In your answer you should refer to Christianity. **(4)**

(Total 20 marks)

Leave blank

Q5

Q6

6 **a)** Keep your definition brief (see p. 52).

b) Take care with this question which asks for a description of how churches help with children (not adults). Pages 54–5 will help you.

c) There are two parts to this answer. First decide what the key points of the Christian ceremony are, then how each of these helps the marriage succeed. When you write the answer say *what* the point is and then *how* it may help (see pp. 48–9). Page 122 gives help in answering **(c)** questions.

d) This is your opportunity to give your views, so you could begin, 'I think... because...'. Give the argument against this, 'Other people think... because...'. Make sure you include a Christian view on cohabiting. Make sure you come to a conclusion and explain it. See pages 42–3 for general information, pages 44–5 for the Christian attitude. Page 123 deals with how to answer **(d)** questions.

4 SOCIAL HARMONY

In this unit you will learn:

- about the growth of equal rights for women in the UK
- about the biblical teachings on the roles of men and women (Genesis 1: 27, Galatians 3: 26–9, Ephesians 5: 21–33, 1 Timothy 2: 9–15)
- about differences among Christians in their attitudes to the roles of men and women, including the role of women in ministry and the reasons for them (equality and sexism)
- the nature of the UK as a multi-ethnic society including prejudice, discrimination and racism
- the teachings of Christianity which help to promote racial harmony, including reference to Luke 10: 25–37, Acts 10: 1–35, Galatians 3: 26–9 and statements by the churches
- the contribution of ONE modern Christian person or organisation to racial harmony and the Christian basis for this work

Figure A *This flower is a completely different colour to those around it. Do you find it ugly or beautiful because of this?*

- the quality, variety and richness of life in the UK as a multi-faith society, including considerations of religious freedom and religious pluralism
- differences among Christians in their attitudes to other religions (exclusivism, inclusivism and pluralism) and the reasons for them.

The key terms you must know the meaning of are:

equality, sexism, multi-ethnic society, prejudice, discrimination, racism, racial harmony, multi-faith society, religious pluralism, religious freedom

ACTIVITY

1. Look at Figure A on this page. Why might some people consider it a metaphor for racism or other forms of prejudice? What do you think it might be saying? Look through a few magazines and choose your own image that could form the basis of a poster or article about discrimination. Explain why you chose that picture and how you plan to use it.

4 Sexism

AIM

To understand the growth of women's rights in the UK.

KEY TERMS

discrimination putting prejudice into practice and treating people less favourably because of their race/gender/colour/class

equality the state of everyone having equal rights regardless of gender/race/class

sexism discriminating against people because of their gender (being male or female)

STARTER

Who would you say this poster (Figure B) was aimed at? What are they supposed to do about the situation?

Prepare your daughter for working life.

Give her less pocket money than your son.

After 30 years of equal pay law, women's wages are still 18% lower than men's. www.eoc.org.uk

EQUAL OPPORTUNITIES COMMISSION

Figure B While a large proportion of women now work, this Equal Opportunities Commission poster suggests that there is still a long way to go before true equality is achieved. Would you agree? Why?

Women's rights in the twentieth century

Sexual **discrimination** against women has been normal practice throughout history. Because of their greater strength, men have dominated society. However, the past hundred years have seen major challenges and changes to this.

- In 1918, women over 31 years of age received the vote, eighty years after it was given to men.
- In 1928, women over 21 years of age were given the vote and permitted to stand for Parliament.
- The First and Second World Wars made a big impact on women because they were given the opportunity to do responsible jobs and demonstrate their capabilities. This was a big step forward in the campaign for sexual **equality**.
- In 1945, women lost out as men returned from the war and needed their jobs back.
- During the 1950s, the government encouraged married women to give up ideas of a career in favour of being housewives and rearing children.

Sexism was regarded as common sense. Men with families should take preference over women in the jobs market. Men should earn more money than women because they had families to support. It was also commonly believed that men were more dependable employees than women who were likely to get pregnant and leave their boss in the lurch.

- The arrival of the contraceptive pill in the 1960s challenged that argument. It signalled the rise of feminism. This also marked a wider change in attitudes; people were beginning to think that everyone, no matter what their gender, race or religion, was entitled to the same rights.
- Various laws were passed to enforce that idea, beginning in 1970 with the Equal Pay Act. This gave women the right to the same pay and benefits as a man doing the same job.
- Five years later, the Sex Discrimination Act made it illegal to discriminate against a person based on their gender or marital status. The Act also set up the Equal Opportunities Commission to ensure the legislation was being carried out.

- Further progress was made with the 1996 Employment Rights Act. This said people could not be unfairly dismissed for reasons such as being pregnant or taking maternity leave. Today the number of women who work is almost equal to the number of men: the big difference is that a large number of women work part-time. Should this make any difference to their rights?

Equality in education

Today we take it for granted that girls are entitled to the same education as boys and the number of women going to university has been steadily rising. Women have emerged with good degrees equalling, and in some cases exceeding, the achievements of men, which has well and truly defeated the old idea that it is wrong to educate girls. The Victorians had reasoned that because a female brain is smaller than a male one, too much education would cause a woman's brain to overheat!

FOR RESEARCH

As a class, build up a list on the board of:
- things which show women have gained equality during the twentieth century
- evidence of women's increasing equality that you have noticed (e.g. women bus-drivers)
- areas where you think there is still room for improvement (check the Equal Opportunities Commission website for evidence by visiting www.heinemann.co.uk/hotlinks, typing in the express code 2280P and clicking on this section)
- areas where you think men do not have equal rights with women (e.g. types of clothing they are expected to wear).

Per cent

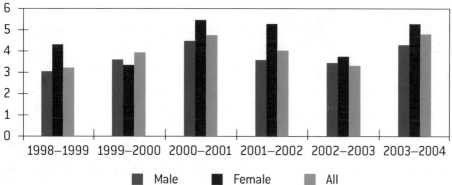

Figure C This graph shows the growth in average weekly earnings of full-time employees in the UK. It allows you to compare the growth experienced by male and female employees.

ACTIVITIES

1. Look at Figure C and other graphs and statistics on the government's website by visiting www.heinemann.co.uk/hotlinks, typing in the express code 2280P and clicking on this section. What do you find the most surprising about women's pay today?

2. With a partner make a list of ten words which could be considered sexist. Here are two to start you off: 'mankind', 'chairman'. Would you say these words are offensive to women or do you think they are used in a fairly neutral way today?

3. Adverts often give a good indication of what is happening in society. Look at some present-day adverts in magazines or on television, and decide whether any are sexist. It is likely that you will be able to find adverts directed against men as well as against women – adverts for new cars are worth studying. Do you think they are harmless fun or sexist? Why?

4 Biblical teachings about the roles of men and women

AIM

To understand some different scripture references to the roles of men and women.

Christian views on the roles of men and women

There is a difference of opinion among Christians today about the roles men and women should play in the life of the Church and in a Christian family. These different views hinge on the interpretations of passages of scripture.

Jesus' treatment of women

The Gospel stories show that Jesus treated women with respect at a time when society was male dominated. It is evident from the scriptures that Jesus did have women among his followers.

- In the account of Jesus' visit to Martha and Mary (Luke 10: 38–42) it is clear that it was unusual for a teacher to allow a woman to learn.
- On other occasions Jesus goes out of his way to show compassion towards women who are suffering by healing them. (Luke 13: 11–13).
- Christians believe it is significant that the first people to see the risen Christ were the women who came to the tomb.

Jesus undoubtedly had many women followers, and some from high levels of society helped to finance his ministry (Luke 8: 1–3), but he chose twelve men to be his apostles to carry on his work. Jesus also specifically gave Peter authority to found the early church and for that reason St Peter is regarded as the first Bishop of Rome.

Figure D *Many Christians regard this episode, when Jesus visited the home of Martha and Mary, as a significant indication of his respect for women. Despite the fact that there was housework to be done, Mary chose to sit near Jesus and learn. When her sister complained that she was lazy, Jesus said Mary had made the right decision. You can read the story in Luke 10: 38–42.*

ACTIVITY

1. Explain why Jesus' treatment of women was unusual for the time.

Biblical teachings

The following quotations, with the exception of A, are taken from the letters St Paul wrote to help members of the early Church.

A *So God created human beings, making them to be like himself. He created them male and female.* (Genesis 1: 27)

B *I also want women to be modest and sensible about their clothes and to dress properly; not with fancy hair styles or with gold ornaments or pearls or expensive dresses, but with good deeds, as is proper for women who claim to be religious. Women should learn in silence and all humility. I do not allow them to teach or to have authority over men; they must keep quiet. For Adam was created first, and then Eve. And it was not Adam who was deceived; it was the woman who was deceived and broke God's law. But a woman will be saved through having children, if she perseveres in faith and love and holiness, with modesty.* (1 Timothy 2: 9–15)

C *Submit yourselves to one another because of your reverence for Christ. Wives submit to your husbands as to the Lord. For a husband has authority over his wife just as the Christ has authority over the church.*

Husbands, love your wives just as Christ loved the church and gave his life for it. He did this to dedicate the church to God by his word, after making it clean by washing it in water in order to present the church to himself in all its beauty – pure and faultless, without spot or wrinkle or any other imperfection. Men ought to love their wives just as they love their own bodies. A man who loves his wife loves himself. (No one ever hates his own body. Instead he feeds it and takes care of it, just as Christ does the church; for we are members of his body.) As the scripture says, 'For this reason a man will leave his father and mother and unite with his wife, and the two will become one'. There is a deep secret truth revealed in this scripture, which I understand as applying to Christ and the church. But it also applies to you; every husband must love his wife as himself, and every wife must respect her husband. (Ephesians 5: 21–33)

D *So there is no difference between Jews and Gentiles, between slaves and free men, between men and women; you are all one in union with Christ Jesus.* (Galatians 3: 27)

ACTIVITIES

2. a) Read quotations A–D and note down what each is saying about the role of men and the role of women. Write down the reason given.
b) What would you say appears to have been St Paul's attitude to the role of women in his society and in the Church? Does he ever waver from that view?
3. Are there any similarities or differences between the teaching of Jesus and St Paul?
4. In quotation B St Paul looks back to the Creation story as evidence that women can lead men astray. Do you see any contradictions between quotations A and B?
5. Using the material on this page, construct a case to argue that women should not take a leading role in church life.
6. Using the material on this page, construct the opposite argument to say that women should take a leading role in church life.

Different attitudes to the roles of men and women among modern Christians

AIM

To understand the differences among Christians in their attitudes to the roles of men and women and the reasons for them, and to understand differences of opinion about the role of women in the ministry.

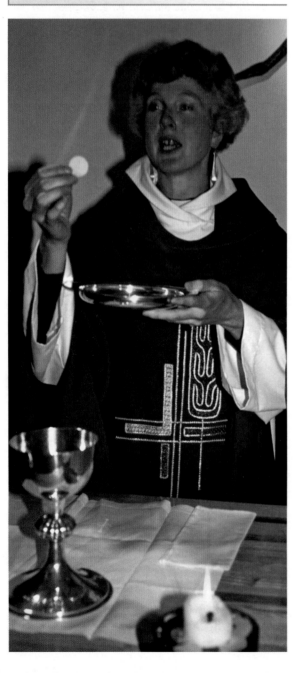

Women in the ministry

- Some Christians believe that women should be allowed into the ministry. They interpret the scriptures to mean that men and women have equal roles in the Church and base their argument on Jesus' treatment of women. They believe it is significant that women were with him at the crucifixion and that Jesus chose to appear first to women after his resurrection. They argue that Jesus only chose male apostles because it would have been totally unacceptable in his day to have female disciples. They feel that it would be just as wrong to prevent women from being ordained as priests today. The majority of Anglicans accept this line of argument.

- There are other Protestant groups that argue that men and women should have different roles in the home and in the Church. They believe that the Bible is the unalterable word of God and should be followed strictly. Their case is based largely on the teachings of St Paul and the fact that Jesus chose twelve male apostles. Although women should attend church, they must remain silent and take no part in its leadership. Only men can be church leaders.

Figure E When women priests were first ordained into the Church of England in 1994, it caused controversy. Some Christians left the Church of England to become Roman Catholics and even today there are parishes that do not want a female vicar. The very successful BBC comedy series starring Dawn French as 'The Vicar of Dibley' took up the theme of the problems encountered by a female vicar. Do you think traditional attitudes to the roles of men and women will eventually disappear? Why?

- Although the Roman Catholic Church believes men and women have equal roles in life they do not think this is the case in church leadership. They point to the fact that Jesus personally nominated Peter to lead the church and become the first Bishop of Rome. The Roman Catholic Catechism states that, 'The Lord Jesus chose men to form the college of the twelve apostles, and the apostles did the same when they chose collaborators to succeed them in their ministry… For this reason the ordination of women is not possible'.

Although women can never be ordained as priests, the Roman Catholic Church explains that they do have a part to play in ministry. 'More laywomen serve in academic positions in colleges and seminaries, as directors of religious education and catechists. They serve as directors of diocesan offices … bishops' assistants, canon lawyers, tribunal members, and in other diocesan administrative positions. In areas where there are few priests or where priests are available only for periodic liturgies, women are administering parishes so that a stable presence of Church is available. Women serve as pastoral ministers, counsellors, hospital chaplains, spiritual directors…' (*The Essential Catholic Handbook*, p. 94)

FOR RESEARCH

List the jobs that women can do in the Roman Catholic Church and find out briefly what each job involves.

The role of men and women in the Christian home

Once again the differences of opinion within the Christian Church about the roles of men and women depend on the interpretation of scripture.

The quotations on page 63 demonstrate that St Paul, who was most influential in the formation of the early Church, held strong views about the roles men and women should play both in the church and in a relationship. Those Christians who believe that the Bible contains the word of God and the literal truth follow St Paul's teachings as closely as possible. More liberal Christians either follow the spirit of Jesus' teachings or interpret the scriptures to suit the times.

- Some Christians, for example evangelical Protestants who follow the Bible literally, believe that a woman's role is as a wife and a mother. She should run a Christian home and obey her husband. The man is the head of the family, the person responsible for providing for the family. His is the superior role in the family. This is based on the teachings of St Paul and the creation story in Genesis in which God created man first while woman was only made out of one of Adam's rib bones.
- The majority of Christians believe men and women should have an equal role in the home. They base their views on the way Jesus treated women, on St Paul's teachings that male and female are equal in Christ (Galatians 3: 27), and on the passage in Genesis that said men and women were created at the same time in the image of God (Genesis 1: 27).

ACTIVITIES

1. Outline the different attitudes among Christians to the role of women in the ministry.
2. Draw two columns and write in each the two different Christian approaches to the roles of men and women in the home. Do not forget to include the reasons.

For discussion
'Christians should always treat men and women equally.' Consider whether all Christians would agree with this statement.

The UK as a multi-ethnic society

AIM

To understand the nature of the United Kingdom as a multi-ethnic society.

KEY TERMS

discrimination putting prejudice into practice and treating people less favourably because of their race/gender/colour/class

multi-ethnic society many different races and cultures living together in one society

prejudice believing some people are inferior or superior without even knowing them

racial harmony different races/colours living together happily

racism the belief that some races are superior to others

STARTER

Look at Figures F and G. Work out what the single largest population group in the UK is at present. What percentage of the population belongs to an ethnic minority group? What is the largest ethnic minority group in the UK?

United Kingdom

	Total population		Non-White population
	(Numbers)	(Percentages)	(Percentages)
White	54,153,898	92.1	-
Mixed	677,117	1.2	14.6
Indian	1,053,411	1.8	22.7
Pakistani	747,285	1.3	16.1
Bangladeshi	283,063	0.5	6.1
Other Asian	247,664	0.4	5.3
All Asian or Asian British	2,331,423	4.0	50.3
Black Caribbean	565,876	1.0	12.2
Black African	485,277	0.8	10.5
Black other	97,585	0.2	2.1
All Black or Black British	1,148,738	2.0	24.8
Chinese	247,403	0.4	5.3
Other ethnic groups	230,615	0.4	5.0
All minority ethnic population	4,635,296	7.9	100.0
All population	58,789,194	100	

Figure F *The population of the United Kingdom by ethnic group, April 2001.*

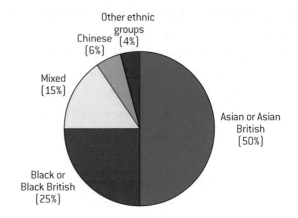

Figure G *The non-white population of the UK by ethnic group, April 2001.*

Multi-ethnic Britain

Some of the tabloid newspapers use sensational headlines and stories to scare people about the number of 'foreigners' coming into Britain. People already living in the UK become frightened that their life will change for the worse. In reality it is very hard to say what a pure British person is like or even if one exists. History shows that the United Kingdom has continually absorbed people of different nationalities, just like every other country.

A good mix of history

There was an influx of Italians in 54 BC when Julius Caesar and the Romans arrived, then came the Anglo-Saxons from Germany, followed by the Vikings from Scandinavia and the French from Normandy and so it goes on. Many settled, married into families already here and merged into our ancestry.

Since 1066 many other groups both large and small arrived in Britain. Some, like the Huguenots from France and the Jews from eastern Europe, were fleeing religious **prejudice** and persecution. Other people arrived to fill job vacancies when the UK did not have a large enough workforce.

In the nineteenth century Queen Victoria's expansion of the British Empire brought the UK into contact with people from outside Europe. When the Empire became the British Commonwealth, immigrant workers were invited to come from India, Pakistan, Bangladesh, Africa and the Caribbean to undertake the jobs no one else wanted.

At the end of the twentieth century a similar situation happened again. This time people from less prosperous areas such as the former Communist countries of eastern Europe, Iraq, China and other parts of the world arrived as migrant workers or asylum seekers fleeing persecution. They have often been prepared to do poorly-paid jobs in catering and fruit picking that many UK residents do not want to do.

Figure H *Boxer Amir Khan is welcomed back to his home town of Bolton after winning a silver medal in the Athens Olympics in 2004. There was great interest in his Olympic success because no one expected a 17-year-old to do so well. Does his religion or ethnic group matter? Why?*

Racism

Discrimination has been around for a long time and different people have found themselves the victims of it over the years. For example, during the eighteenth century slave traders thought of black people as animals that could be made to work for them. This prevented the traders having a conscience about the way they treated their fellow human beings. Their attitude affected the treatment of anyone who did not look or sound like them. Nowadays, most people agree that **racism** is evil. It creates hatred and can lead to violence such as riots. Violence never solves the problems, it just makes the situation worse.

The 1976 Race Relations Act

This act made it illegal to discriminate against people on grounds of race, colour, nationality, ethnic or national origin, in terms of housing, training, jobs, education or the provision of services. It is illegal to use threatening, abusive or insulting words in public or to publish anything that could stir up racial hatred. The Commission for Racial Equality was also set up to stop race discrimination.

Racial harmony

Too often it is the negative side of a **multi-ethnic society** that makes the news. The advantages of a multi-ethnic society are overlooked.

- The UK has a wide variety of music, culture, food and clothes from the different cultures.
- New ideas arrive in the UK with new people.
- It can make for a more peaceful world as people of different races and nationalities learn to live and work alongside each other.
- It is good for religions to see members of different ethnic groups following their religion.

FOR RESEARCH

Find out about the influence that different nationalities or ethnic groups have had on music or fashion.

ACTIVITY

1. Write a reasoned reply to a magazine letter that complains Britain is being weakened by foreigners arriving to live here. Remember to include the benefits that can come from living in a multi-ethnic society.

AIM

To understand the nature of multi-faith Britain and evaluate its strengths and weaknesses.

STARTER

The people on this spread belong to an interfaith group. They come from many different religions but are united by their desire to understand each other's religion better and to foster good relations between those religions. What do you think they hope to get out of this? Look at the list of key terms on this page and choose the one you think best describes this group's attitude to other faiths.

KEY TERMS

multi-faith society many different religions living together in one society
religious freedom the right to practise your religion and change your religion
religious pluralism accepting all religions as having an equal right to coexist

Religious freedom

During the twentieth century, Britain has increasingly become a **multi-faith society** and, unlike some parts of the world, religious groups do on the whole exist peacefully side by side in the UK. Although Britain is recognised as a Christian country, there is complete **religious freedom** for people to belong to whatever faith they like, or none at all.

I really look forward to the visits we make, and it's not just the food! However, I do admit to having fond memories of that Jewish social evening we went to; there was a fantastic honey cake Eve made – it was out of this world! We were able to chat to members of the faith about their beliefs and ask questions without fear of causing offence. It was really informative. I never understood about **circumcision** before. You wouldn't normally walk up to a Jew and ask them, would you? But in an informal situation like this we felt we could discuss anything. And actually the Muslims in our group were able to add their comments on circumcision too.

It was great for us. We're a very tiny religion, so it's good to have the chance to tell people what we are about. No, we're not trying to convert anybody, we respect their views. And if you think about it, people who choose to join an interfaith group like this are already happy and confident in their own religion. It's just that we don't get many opportunities to explain our philosophies. I think it makes for more peace and tolerance in society if people can get together like this and talk.

Liz is a Roman Catholic.

Paul is a member of the Baha'i faith.

It was our festival of Baisakhi coming up so my community was keen that the interfaith group come and join in. I think most of them didn't know what to expect! We got more from their visit than we expected because of all the questions. It's interesting how some questions really make you think about what you believe. It is so easy to trot out the standard answers, but when someone quizzes you further you have to really consider things. Does it weaken my faith? No, not at all. You could say it strengthens it because it challenges me to think very seriously why I believe something.

The interfaith group does not just go and visit the religion that is having the biggest feast! We also go to people's place of worship and join them for normal worship. No, I do not have any problem with that. God is God as far as I am concerned, whether I join Muslim women in the women's gallery at the mosque or sit in the synagogue I feel I can still join in prayer in my heart. I admit that I do not always know what the words are. My Hebrew is like my Arabic – non-existent! But that's no problem. I really felt we were all joining together to worship God.

Baljinder is a Sikh.

Ann is a Christian and a member of the local Salvation Army.

I am all for groups like this. Too often people do not really understand what Muslims believe. I was really pleased when the interfaith group said they wanted to visit the mosque and talk to people. The Muslim community was delighted to welcome them; somebody said afterwards that they did not realise how much we all had in common. Now that's a really positive step, isn't it?

Asma is a Muslim.

ACTIVITIES

1. Read the comments from the interfaith group members and make a list of all the things they have gained from a multi-faith society.

2. Make a list of the difficulties that could arise from living in a multi-faith society.

3. How does the interfaith group attempt to put **religious pluralism** into practice?

4 Christian views on racial harmony and religious freedom

AIM

To understand the attitude of Christians towards other religions and the teachings of Christianity which help to promote racial harmony.

KEY TERMS

prejudice believing some people are inferior or superior without even knowing them

racial harmony different races/colours living together happily

racism the belief that some races are superior to others

religious freedom the right to practise your religion and change your religion

St Paul taught Christians that people of other races and religions were equal in the eyes of God. Read what he wrote to members of the early Church.

It is through faith that all of you are God's sons in union with Christ Jesus. You were baptised into union with Christ, and now you are clothed, so to speak, with the life of Christ himself. So there is no difference between Jews and Gentiles, between slaves and free men, between men and women; you are all one in union with Christ Jesus. (Galatians 3: 26–8)

It is because believers share a love of Jesus that they are equal, St Paul says.

Figure I *Some people were surprised when the Reverend Dr John Sentamu was appointed Bishop of Birmingham in 2002. Christians, however, should not have had any difficulty accepting his appointment since the Bible makes it clear that prejudice is totally unacceptable.*

ACTIVITY

1. Read the story in Acts 10: 35 that caused Peter to say these words. 'I now realise that it is true that God treats everyone on the same basis. Those who worship him and do what is right are acceptable to him, no matter what race they belong to.' Acts (10: 34–6)

a) Jews like Peter would not normally associate closely with non-Jews, so how did God persuade Peter to think differently about non-Jews?

b) What implications does this passage have for the way Christians should treat other races?

Christianity and racial harmony

The Bible opens with a description of God creating humans in his own image, therefore, Christians believe that everyone should be respected as God's creation. This means prejudice and racism are wrong. There are many more teachings in the Old and the New Testaments which reinforce this, for example the story of the Good Samaritan (Luke 10: 25–37).

ACTIVITY

2. Read the story Jesus told about the Good Samaritan in Luke 10: 25–37.
a) What races are involved and how does each treat the other?
b) Why is this story seen as important in teaching about Christian attitudes to racism?

The Christian attitude to other religions

Most modern Christians believe that people should be free to follow whatever religion they like, or none at all. There are, however, three different Christian approaches to religious freedom.

Exclusivism: As the word suggests, some people are excluded from heaven. Jesus said, 'I am the way, the truth, and the life; no one goes to the Father except by me' (John 14: 6). Some Christians believe this means only those who follow Christianity will go to heaven. Other religions have gone wrong so it would be right to try to convert a non-believer to Christianity.

Inclusivism: Some Christians believe that while all religions can help people to reach God, only Christianity has the complete answer. This is because Jesus taught that people should believe in him to get to heaven, and only Christians believe in Jesus as the Son of God. This is often the view held by Roman Catholic Christians. While other faiths should be respected, the right path should be explained to them.

Pluralism: As the word suggests, there are many religions. Some Christians believe that all religions will lead to God, none is superior and none is wrong. People are free to follow the way that suits them best. These Christians do not regard the Bible as 'the word of God', but rather as holy writings like many other sacred books. These Christians do not think they should try to persuade people to change their religion. They say Jesus never tried to convert the Jews in his society and on one occasion he explained to his followers, 'There are many rooms in my Father's house, and I am going to prepare a place for you' (John 14: 2). This is interpreted to mean there are places for people from all religions.

For discussion

Do you think a Christian who firmly believes their religion is the correct one, has a duty to convert others?

ACTIVITIES

3. Explain the three different Christian approaches to other religions. Be sure to include the reasons for each group's beliefs.
4. What implications do you think these views have for a Christian considering missionary work?
5. Read the account of St Paul visiting Athens in Acts 17: 22–3. Which of the three approaches to religious freedeom – exclusivism, inclusivism or pluralism – does it support. Why?
6. With a partner, role-play a discussion between a Christian who believes other faiths have the right to practise their faith if they want to and a Christian who believes other faiths have got it wrong.

AIM

To understand the work of Martin Luther King and Archbishop Desmond Tutu to promote racial harmony and the Christian basis for their work.

STARTER

Read this famous extract from a speech by Martin Luther King. As a class, discuss what his words have to do with Christian attitudes towards racism. (To remind yourself look at pages 70–1.)

I have a dream that one day … all of God's children, black men and white men, Jews and Gentiles, Protestants and Catholics will be able to join hands and sing in the words of the old Negro spiritual, 'Free at last! Free at last! Thank God Almighty, we are free at last!'

Figure J *Martin Luther King was inspired by his religious beliefs to speak out against prejudice. Have you ever been inspired to stand up for something as a result of your beliefs?*

Martin Luther King

Martin Luther King was a black Baptist minister who campaigned to stop the racial segregation of black people in America. At that time in the early 1960s, black people were not allowed the vote, not allowed to go to the same places as white people and earned half the amount of money most white people did. King bravely spoke out against these injustices and became the leader of the Civil Rights Movement in America.

What did he do?

One famous incident of racial discrimination involved a black woman, Rosa Parkes, who had paid for her seat on the bus. She was then told to get up and stand at the back because a white man wanted to sit down. When she refused, she was arrested. Although this sort of thing had happened countless times before, it proved to be the final straw. The black community rose up in protest. Martin Luther King persuaded them to wage a campaign of peaceful resistance, urging black people not to use the buses at all, which would result in the bus companies losing huge sums of money. After many years of non-violent protests, America changed the law in 1965 and segregation was ended.

Why did he do it?

King was sure that God was on the side of the poor and the oppressed. He drew inspiration from the story of Moses leading the Israelites out of slavery in Egypt with God's help.

FOR RESEARCH

Find out more information about Martin Luther King's campaign and prepare a presentation for a year group. Remember to show how King drew inspiration from Christianity.

Archbishop Desmond Tutu

Desmond Tutu was born in South Africa in 1931 at a time when black people were treated as inferior to white people. They were banned from using the same facilities as white people, paid low wages and housed in appalling conditions. Tutu trained as a priest and did a degree in the UK where he saw that black and white people could live and work alongside each other.

What did he do?

When Desmond Tutu returned to South Africa as a priest, he resisted the call to fight white supremacy with violence and terrorism. Tutu was convinced that God was on the side of black people in their struggle for equality, and that justice would eventually come to South Africa.

Despite the difficulties and dangers, Tutu spoke publicly about racial injustices and led many peaceful marches. He was imprisoned many times. However, in 1986 he became the first black Archbishop of South Africa and used his position to make the world pay attention to the appalling treatment black people received. He persuaded countries around the world not to buy South African produce such as fruit. This resulted in the white government losing so much money that they were forced to take notice of Tutu and black South Africans.

In 1994, after a very long struggle, South Africa held the first elections in which black people could vote. As a result Nelson Mandela became the first black president of the country. Archbishop Tutu was put in charge of a commission to examine all the miscarriages of justice in South Africa in the past. Tutu surprised everyone by encouraging people to tell the truth and seek forgiveness from their victims.

Why did he do it?

Like Martin Luther King, Desmond Tutu believed God would lead the oppressed black people to freedom in the same way as he had led the Israelites out of Egypt. Tutu was also sure that Jesus preached love, not violence, as the way to solve problems so Tutu used methods of peaceful protest. Because Jesus forgave his enemies from the cross, Tutu was inspired to think about forgiveness rather than trial and punishment when the new government took over.

ACTIVITIES

1. What is Archbishop Tutu saying here about the Christian attitude to racism?
If it were not for faith, I am certain lots of us would have been hate-filled and bitter ... But to speak of God, you must speak of your neighbour ... He does not tolerate a relationship with himself that excludes your neighbour.
2. Summarise the contribution of one individual Christian to **racial harmony**. What was the Christian basis for his or her work?

Figure K Desmond Tutu challenged a rule which said that only white people could use this beach. In 1989, he peacefully led a group of black people onto the beach, but they were chased off by white police with whips. The event caused outrage around the world. Why do you think this was the case?

SOCIAL HARMONY

ACTIVITIES

1. Design a poster showing the different views Christians hold about the role of men and women in the Church.

2. In pairs, prepare a presentation showing the different ideas Christians have about other religions. Make sure you support your comments with evidence.

3. Collect pictures from magazines and newspapers to create a display that illustrates the strengths of a multi-ethnic society.

4. What are the advantages of living in a multi-ethnic society?

5. Test yourself and a partner on the meanings of the key terms on page 59. Write each one on a slip of paper. Look back through this unit of work to find the meaning and write it on a separate slip of paper. In pairs, see how quickly and accurately you can match each word to its meaning.

Tackling an exam question

Here is a **(d)** question from the exam paper.

> *'In a multi-faith society, Christians should not try to convert followers of other religions.'*
>
> Do you agree? Give reasons for your opinion, showing you have considered another point of view. **(4)**   *(Edexcel Unit B, 2004)*

Planning your answer to this question

1. The **(d)** question is the evaluation question. It is the only time the examiner asks you what you actually think about an issue.
2. Do not forget that you are also being asked what people who disagree with you will say.
3. Look at page 123 for more help on tackling **(d)** questions.

Student's answer

I agree. In a multi-faith society people going round trying to convert others to their religion is only going to cause trouble. ✓ (Level 1) *The others might be quite happy with their own religion and do not want any interference. They will say that they will go to heaven if they lead a good life. It's a free world and people ought to be able to believe what they want to. Also it might start fights if people keep pushing their religion at others.* ✓ (Level 2)

Examiner's comments

The student offered her opinion very clearly at the beginning with a reason (Level 1) and she went on to offer other reasons to support it, which took her up to Level 2. But she never told us what Christians think about the subject, nor did she mention another point of view – why some people think you should try to convert people in a multi-faith society. If she had offered that viewpoint her answer might have gone up a level. To reach Level 4 she needs to show a full understanding of the issue and reach a personal conclusion.

Level 1 (1 mark)

For a point of view supported by one relevant reason.

Level 2 (2 marks)

For a basic for and against, or a reasoned opinion, or well argued points of view with no personal opinion.

Level 3 (3 marks)

For a reasoned personal opinion, using religious/moral argument, referring to another point of view.

Level 4 (4 marks)

For a coherent, reasoned personal opinion, using religious/moral argument, evaluating another point of view to reach a personal conclusion.

Student's improved answer

I agree. In a multi-faith society people going round trying to convert others to their religion is only going to cause trouble. ✓ (L1) The others might be quite happy with their own religion and do not want any interference. They will say that they will go to heaven if they lead a good life. It's a free world and people ought to be able to believe what they want to. Also it might start fights if people keep pushing their religion at others. ✓ (L2)

Christians might say you should try to convert people to Christianity because Jesus said the way to God was through him. That would give them the chance to follow the correct path to God. ✓ (L3) The only problem could be that there are lots of religions in a multi-faith society and if everyone was going round trying to convert people, things could get out of hand. I think it is better if Christians welcome people who want to learn about their religion, but do not go out searching for converts because then no one will feel under pressure to believe in something they do not want to believe in. ✓ (L4)

7 a) Clear definition required (see p. 68).

b) Take care to answer about different religions not races. You need to briefly discuss the three main approaches (see p. 71).

c) Another what and why question. Explain what the person or organisation has done and why each action helped racial harmony. Pages 72–3 provide information about the work of two people. Help with this sort of question is found on page 122.

d) Give your personal opinion and say why you think that. Then give the opposite viewpoint and the reasons for that. Pages 68–9 will give you general help. Be sure you have said what Christians would say and why (see pp. 70–1). Make sure you come to a conclusion. Page 123 will help with this sort of evaluative answer.

Question 7(b) is based on a question from Edexcel Unit B paper 2004. Question 7(c) is taken from Edexcel Unit B paper 2003. Questions 8(b) and 8(c) are taken from the Edexcel Unit B paper 2004.

Leave blank

SECTION FOUR: SOCIAL HARMONY

You must answer ONE question from this section.

EITHER QUESTION 7

7 a) What is a *multi-faith society*? **(2)**

b) Outline Christian attitudes towards other religions. **(6)**

c) Explain how **ONE** modern Christian person or organisation has promoted racial harmony. **(8)**

d) *'You can't expect people to live together peacefully in a multi-faith society.'*
Do you agree? Give reasons for your opinion, showing you have considered another point of view. In your answer you should refer to Christianity. **(4)**

(Total 20 marks)

Q7

OR QUESTION 8

8 a) What is *prejudice*? **(2)**

b) Outline Christian teachings which help to promote racial harmony. **(6)**

c) Explain why there are different attitudes to the roles of men and women in Christianity. **(8)**

d) *'A multi-ethnic society is the best way forward for everyone.'*
Do you agree? Give reasons for your opinion, showing you have considered another point of view. In your answer you should refer to Christianity. **(4)**

(Total 20 marks)

Q8

---

8 a) Keep your definition brief (see p. 66).

b) Give a brief account of Christian teachings on racial harmony (see pp. 70–1).

c) There are two parts to this answer (see pp. 62–3). *What* are the different attitudes and *why*. Page 122 gives help with **(c)** questions.

d) Your views are requested so you could begin, 'I think... because...'. Then give the other side's views, 'Other people think... because...'. Make sure that you have explained how Christianity would react to this statement (see pp. 70–1). Page 123 will help you answer a **(d)** question. Conclude with your opinion and the reasons that support it.

In this chapter you will learn:

- about the variety and range of specifically religious programmes (religious broadcasts) in terms of general contents and how to assess the reasons for a programme's popularity/unpopularity
- how *either* TV soap operas *or* the national daily press deal with religious and moral issues of importance to Christians by studying their handling of one issue in-depth

Figure A *The BBC filming an episode of their popular religious broadcast* Songs of Praise.

- how a specifically religious theme(s) of importance to Christians is explored in a film *or* TV drama. This will include an understanding of why the theme is important, how it was dealt with, whether the treatment was fair to religious people and how the treatment of the theme could have been improved
- about the way religion is dealt with in the media in general and how to make a personal evaluation.

Useful concepts

Religious issues involve discussions about life and ultimate questions such as 'Why am I here?' or 'What happens when I die?' which religions may attempt to answer. Alternatively, more straightforward questions to do with the practices of one particular religious group such as 'Can a Christian marry a divorcee?' or 'Should priests be celibate?' are also considered to be religious issues.

Moral issues are likely to be concerned with whether an action is right or wrong. Although the religions will have something to say about it, people who do not believe in any religion are also likely to have opinions about what is right and wrong. Issues such as abortion and stealing could be considered moral issues. These are also sometimes referred to as ethical issues.

ACTIVITY

1. Go to the BBC's website by visiting www.heinemann.co.uk/hotlinks, typing in the express code 2280P and clicking on this section. Print their 'Religion and Ethics TV and Radio Schedules' for the coming weekend. Analyse the programmes according to:

a) which religion is covered

b) whether the programme is on radio or television, has a worship content, religious news, religious music, moral comment or other relevant material

c) whether you think the coverage of the different religions is balanced or not.

5 The media

AIM

To understand what the mass media are and the effect they can have on religious and moral issues of interest to Christians.

STARTER

With a partner, discuss what is meant by 'the mass media'. Think about:

- who are the mass?
- what are the media?
- how important are the mass media in our society today?
- could the mass media ever be dangerous?

It is easier now to communicate than it has ever been. We can soon discover what is going on in another part of the world and just as quickly let somebody there know our views. Without question we are the best-informed people in history.

The words 'mass media' refer to the many forms of communication we possess, such as radio, television, newspapers and films. The spider diagram on the opposite page illustrates many of these forms.

When someone talks about 'the mass media' the word mass is simply referring to the masses of people who have access to information.

This chapter looks at the way that the media portray religion and religious and moral issues. You have gained a lot of knowledge about Christianity during your GCSE study so you will be using that knowledge to examine how fair the media are.

How fair is the media?

Most forms of media have another agenda. They are there to make money for the people who own them. The press are there to sell newspapers and magazines and so they are always looking for ways to get us to buy their publications. Films and videos are generally doing the same; they must grab our attention so that we will part with our money. You might think television and radio are different, but they too have to reach large audiences to ensure their survival. We must watch to see if they have distorted stories to grab our attention, played for a laugh at the expense of the truth, made a scandal out of nothing, or been downright prejudiced in order to boost sales.

Figure B *How many different forms of communication can you see in this everyday scene?*

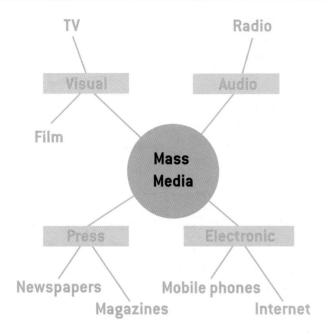

TV

Radio

Visual

Audio

Film

Mass Media

Press

Electronic

Newspapers

Mobile phones

Magazines

Internet

ACTIVITIES

1. Draw two columns and in one list the benefits of having so many forms of media. In the other column list the problems and dangers the media create.

2. a) Copy the diagram above. Add any further forms of communication you can think of.

b) Against each form of communication, write the age group you think is most influenced by this type (e.g. 0–9, 10–19, 20–29 etc.).

c) Which form of communication do you think is the most influential? Why?

d) Which would you say is the most trustworthy, and which the least?

e) Which media do you think are most likely to have an impact on a religious or moral issue? Why?

Using the topic for coursework

You may have chosen to deal with this topic as coursework and pages 117–18 will give you specific help on writing your coursework. If you are using 'Religion and the media' as a coursework option, the following pages will guide you through the way to approach your study of each aspect of the media. Remember that this area of study carries a large proportion of your final mark, so you must give it a great deal of care and attention. You have to write 1500 words, and marks will be awarded for the quality of your written communication in this section as well.

Answering questions on the exam paper

If you are answering questions on the exam paper about 'Religion and the media', the following pages will guide you through the way to approach each aspect of the study. You are free to choose whatever TV programme, newspaper or film that you, or your teacher, think best answers the question and is easiest for you to access. Within each area of study, one particular example has been chosen, but it is only there for guidance on how to focus the analysis of your personal choice. Remember that this is the 'Extended Writing' part of the exam paper where you are advised to spend half an hour on an answer. There are only three parts to the questions here but each carries a lot of marks. In addition there are 3 marks at stake for the quality of your written communication.

ACTIVITIES

3. As a class, decide what the word '**propaganda**' means.

4. What has propaganda got to do with the mass media?

For discussion

In pairs, discuss how religion might be involved with propaganda. Do you think it is acceptable for religions to use the media to promote their ideas? What good could it do? What harm could it do?

RELIGION AND THE MEDIA

AIM

To understand the diversity of the national daily press and evaluate the way it handles religious and moral issues of interest to Christians.

ACTIVITIES

1. Copy down each headline and write alongside whether it deals with a religious or an ethical issue (or possibly both).

2. Look at the three headlines about Madonna's visit to Israel (one appears in the newspaper extract below). Which do you think is the most neutral of the three? Give reasons for your answer.

Priest in choirboy sex scandal

MADONNA VISITS JEWISH PROPHET'S GRAVE

Pilgrims crushed on Hajj

Singer off key: Madonna in mystical mood dismays strict Jews

Investors urge drug companies to help world's poor

CRUCIFIXES BANNED IN SCHOOLS

Vicar steals bishop's wife

Pupils want prayer room in school

It's Madge-ic

MADONNA emerges smiling but teary-eyed from her pilgrimage to a Jerusalem cemetery yesterday.

The star, 46, and hubby Guy Ritchie, 36, joined 2,000 other Kabbalah followers for an emotional ceremony at the grave of mystic Rabbi Yehuda Ashlag.

Madonna, sporting a letter E pendant for her Hebrew name Esther, was guarded by cops as she chanted and prayed. She believes the trip will help wishes come true.
Picture: REX

Some people say that nobody reads newspapers today, but with sales of around ten million copies a day that is clearly not the case. Think how quick celebrities and politicians are to sue a newspaper if it prints a story they do not like. Clearly, many people do read newspapers and plenty of people think that what they say does matter.

We need to find out how newspapers deal with religious and moral issues. To remind yourself of the difference between a religious issue and a moral or ethical issue, look back to the definitions on page 77.

Newspapers report on real life situations – or do they?

This is where the trouble starts! Generally speaking, newspapers do report on real life events. Unlike soap operas and films, in which characters and their actions are invented by the script writer; the stories in newspapers are true. However, there have been cases of newspapers inventing a story or reporting on something that never happened quite like that. Celebrities and politicians have been upset to find themselves at the heart of a smear campaign based on nothing in particular.

This happens because newspapers have to sell themselves. You have only got to look on a shelf in the supermarket or newsagents to see the number and range of papers for sale. That means that each paper has got to find a way of grabbing people's attention. There will always be the regular readers who buy a copy of the *Sun* as they get off the bus, or have a copy of the *Independent* pushed through their letterbox every morning. But equally there are plenty of people who buy whatever they fancy, or whichever headline catches their attention. That means the headlines must be sensational, sometimes at the expense of the truth.

The in-depth study

You are required to make an in-depth study of the press. The best way to do this is to select a particular day and buy four different newspapers. You can begin your study working in twos or fours, because it is often helpful to discuss your thoughts with others.

Choose:

- one from *The Times,* the *Guardian,* the *Independent* or the *Daily Telegraph.*
- one from the *Daily Mail* or the *Daily Express*
- one from the *Sun* or the *Daily Mirror*
- and one from the same day's evening paper.

This will give you a good range of styles and readership.

- Go through the papers and decide what sort of people are likely to be regular readers of each paper. What is their age, gender, typical job?
- Study each paper and briefly note the details of every story that involves an issue of importance to Christians. Then do the same for each story that involves a moral issue that Christians would be interested in.
- What do you notice about the different papers you studied? Could that fit in with the type of people who read this paper and what might interest or not interest them?
- Select the same four stories that involve a religious or moral issue which appeared in all your papers.
- Design a grid like the one shown in the activity box below so you can compare results. Analyse and record the different treatment the story gets in each paper. Compare the prominence it is given in each paper (buried in the middle or on the front). Compare headlines, pictures, use of language in the main article, how much space is devoted to it. Compare the way the story is handled. Do you think the reporting is fairly neutral, or is it encouraging the reader to think this is a good or a bad thing? (Spend some time on this and pinpoint the evidence that leads you to that conclusion.)

Now use the evidence gathered to do the activity.

ACTIVITY

3. Explain how a religious or moral issue of importance to Christians has been dealt with in the national daily press.

Story about ....

Newspaper title	Page number in newspaper	Number of column inches	Picture yes/no	Headline	Use of language	How story was handled
A						
B						
C						
D						

To understand what a soap opera is and study in-depth the way it handles a religious or moral issue of interest to Christians.

STARTER

Everybody talks about watching 'soaps', but what exactly are they? With a partner, make a list of all the TV soaps you can think of. Then try to write a dictionary definition of a soap opera. When you have finished, pool all your answers with members of the class and decide on one definition between you.

The idea for soap operas originally came from America. This kind of serial was aimed mainly at women viewers, so for that reason soap powder manufacturers decided to sponsor them in order to get a good market for their advertising.

Some people are very dismissive of soaps saying, 'I do not watch that sort of thing', but soaps are enormously popular. It is claimed that programmes such as *Coronation Street* can attract an audience of thirteen million viewers each night.

What do we mean by a soap opera?

What makes a soap different from a television play is that it is an ongoing serial which never reaches a conclusion. Different episodes may well be shown three or four times a week, with several storylines running at the same time. There is always the same regular set of characters with guest appearances from other people. The characters live in a small community, often several of them are interrelated and they have to deal with everyday, real-life issues. Viewers get to know the characters well and are interested to watch how they handle the various issues that arise.

HINT

Make sure you are clear what a soap is. Check with your teacher that your choice of study is really a soap. You will lose marks if you answer a question with information about a programme that is not a soap opera. Some examples of soap operas are *Eastenders*, *Coronation Street* and *Emmerdale*. Series such as *Ballykissangel*, *The Vicar of Dibley* and *Holby City*, however, are TV dramas rather than soap operas (see pages 90–1).

Figure C *This is a still from* Eastenders. *The photo shows Jane and Ian whose relationship began to develop before the death of Jane's terminally ill husband. Was Jane wrong to have feelings for Ian?*

The positive side of soaps

- Viewers can learn about real-life issues from watching them.
- There is often a helpline number broadcast at the end of the episode so people can get more advice if they need it.
- Soaps show issues from several viewpoints because, as the story unfolds, you see them through the eyes of different characters. This can be helpful in promoting understanding and awareness of an issue.
- Because many people watch soaps, issues get talked about in public. Not only do people chat to each other about the plot at work, at school and at home, but sometimes issues on programmes are discussed on the radio or in magazines.
- Soaps are not frightened of raising some controversial issues that people might be scared to talk about e.g. alcoholism, arranged marriages, teenage pregnancy, incest, homosexuality, terminal illness, a crisis of religious beliefs, euthanasia.
- No matter what difficulties the characters face, good usually triumphs over evil in the stories, so soaps have a feel-good effect on people.

The negative side of soaps

- They are only stories, not real life. Some people get so involved that they cannot sort fact from fiction and that can be dangerous. There are magazines devoted to soaps containing interviews with characters, and some newspapers even have updates on the story as though the characters really exist.
- Soap operas can exaggerate everyday life. Lots of things happen to a small group of people. Some viewers forget it is not real and might become dissatisfied, thinking their own lives are boring.
- There is always a crisis, which can portray a false view of reality.

ACTIVITIES

1. Think of one positive and one negative aspect of soaps to add to each of the lists on the left.

2. Choose one soap and watch it regularly for two to four weeks. Write down the name of the soap you are studying. Note all the issues that were raised. Analyse them and categorise them as either moral issues or religious issues (look at page 77 if you cannot remember the difference). Then choose one issue (religious or moral) that you know would be of interest to a Christian to base your work on.

- What was the issue?
- Who were the main characters involved in that issue?
- How did the soap deal with it?
- How many different people's views were shown in the soap? Did you think that it was a good rounded view of the problem or was there another aspect they should have shown?
- Why do you think they chose to highlight this issue? Is it topical? Is it an issue people do not find easy to talk about? Would you say a lot of people are faced with this sort of problem? Is it difficult to know the right answer to a situation like this?
- Overall, how well do you think the soap handled this issue? Was it fair in its treatment, or did you feel the soap made it sensational? In what ways do you think it could have been dealt with better?
- You might find useful information for a coursework study on the Internet. Check whether the soap opera has a website with comments about the storyline or the issues raised. You might find some useful comments on the handling of that issue in a magazine.

HINT

Focus on the moral or religious issue – not the soap! That means do not get involved in lengthy explanations of the story.

RELIGION AND THE MEDIA

AIM

To understand the variety and range of programmes about religion on television.

Sunday 12 TELEVISION

BBC1	BBC2	ITV1	Channel 4
6.0 Breakfast (T) (S) *92989473* **8.10** Match Of The Day (T) (S) (R) *8937763* **9.30** Breakfast With Frost (T) (S) *76831* **10.30** The Heaven And Earth Show (S) *59676* **11.30** Countryfile (T) (S) *76218* **12.30** The Politics Show (T) (S) *20164* **1.30** FILM **Herbie Goes Bananas** (Vincent J McEveey, 1980) (T) Wonder what Herbie would make of the congestion charge? More car-with-personality adventures starring Cloris Leachman, Charles Martin Smith, John Vernon, Stephen W Burns, Elyssa Davalos, Joaquin Garay, Harvey Korman. *72980* **3.0** EastEnders (T) (S) *33074763* **4.50** Keeping Up Appearances (T) (S) (R) *1303218* **5.20** Points Of View (T) (S) *3416611* **5.35** Songs Of Praise (T) (S) *962270*	**6.0 CBeebies:** Teletubbies (T) (S) (R) *2629909* **6.40** The Story Makers (T) (S) (R) *4745367* **7.0** CBBC: Tom And Jerry Kids (T) (R) *9404270* **7.20** Looney Tunes (T) (R) *6736831* **7.30** Smile (T) (S) *834473* **10.30** Young Indiana Jones Cronicles (T) (S) *8882473* **11.55** Trade Secrets (T) (R) *7761589* **12.05** The Fresh Prince Of Bel-Air (T) (S) (R) *8926386* **12.30** Wildlife On Two (T) (S) (R) *17473* **1.0** The Future Is Wild (T) (S) *46034* **1.30** Sunday Grandstand: (T) (S) Sport Plus *27491928* **1.50** Racing From Goodwood And Longchamps *47207305* **3.30** Cycling *2029473* **4.50** The Big Interview: Tanni Grey-Thompson *1025218* **5.10** Wildlife On Two (T) (S) (R) *8513638* **5.40** Wild (T) (S) *612251* **5.50** FILM **The Robe** (Henry Koster, 1953) (T) Bibical drama starring Richard Burton, Jean Simmons, Victor Mature. *29189980*	**6.0 GMTV** (T) *3736305* **6.0** News (T) *2231763* **6.10** The Sunday Programme (T) *5364218* **7.30** Diggin' It *4474725* **8.25** Up On The Roof (T) *1505763* **9.25** CITV: UP2U (T) (S) *8690270* **9.55** How 2 (T) (S) (R) *9238589* **10.10** Finger Tips (T) (S) *9479744* **10.30** The Championship (T) (S) *89102* **11.0** My Favourite Hymns (T) (S) *39744* **12.0** ITV News; (T) (S) Weather *3984034* **12.05** London Today; (T) (S) Weather *3983305* **12.10** F1: Italian Grand Prix (T) (S) *30725928* **3.10** Goodwood Revival (S) *1758909* **4.10** Car Hunt (T) (S) *2006164* **4.40** London Tonight; (T) (S) Weather *1092980* **4.55** FILM **Tucker: The Man And His Dream** (Francis Fod Coppola, 1988) (T) (S) Drama in which Jeff Bridges finds big business getting in the way of his car empire. With Joan Allen, Martin Landau, Christian Slater, Frederic Forrest, Mako, Dean Stockwell, Lloyd Bridges. *52969541*	**6.15 The Hoobs** Iver Five-O (T) (R) *4232386* **6.40** The Hoobs (T) (R) *8815947* **7.05** Speedway *7342725* **8.0** Racing Rivals *75909* **8.30** Freesport On 4 *67980* **9.0** T4 Friends (T) (R) *81560* **9.30** Popworld (T) *2355893* **10.25** Hollyoaks (T) Abby is furious when she hears what's happened to Zara. *95771676* **12.50** Faking It: The T4 Specials (T) Can a history student fake it as a graffiti artist? *9664015* **2.05** The OC (T) The gang head to Palm Springs for some parent-free fun. Not a recipe for disaster or anything. *4419183* **3.05** Collateral: T4 Movie Special (T) Behind the scenes with Tom Cruise, Michael Mann, Jamie Foxx and Jada Pinkett Smith. *9233744* **3.35** Smallville: Superman The Early Years (T) Jonathan gets powered up thanks to Clark's Kryptonian dad. *7715386* **4.35** Stargate SG-1 (T) *7606831* **5.30** Wreck Detectives (T) Dredging for a 17th century warship. *82218*
6.15 Last Of The Summer Wine (T) (S) (R) *190763* **6.45 Antiques Roadshow** Haltwhistle (T) (S) A letter written by JRR Tolkien, fittings from the Titanic's sister ship, and a Roman coin found near Hadrian's Wall. *844560* **7.35 News;** (T) Regional News; Weather *356744*		**6.45 ITV News;** (T) (S) Weather *499638* **7.0 Emmerdale** (T) (S) Debbie confesses she is upset that Cain has gone away without telling her. *8725* **7.30 Coronation Street** (T) (S) Things aren't going well for factory girl Kelly. *183*	**6.35 Scrapheap Challenge** (T) Glaswegians the Irn Cru take on Bath rickshaw drivers Maximus as they battle to create the best dam-busting machines from junk in just 10 hours. *35812* **7.30 News** (T) Including sport and weather. *725*
8.0 Casualty The Ties That Bind Us – Part Two (T) (S) Harry breaks the news that Nina's daring rescue may have devastating consequences. Lucy Benjamin guest stars. *8299* **9.0** PREVIEW **Silent Witness** Death by Water – Part One (T) (S) Leo and Harry's professional rivalry erupts following Sam's departure. Tom Ward and William Gaminara star. Continues tomorrow. *1763*	**8.0 Get A New Life** Canada (T) (S) Problems emerge as Paul Doody and Toni Syrett attempt to relocate to Canada. *9541* **9.0 Crisis Command: Could You Run The Country?** Flood – One (T) (S) Three contestants are given the chance to run the country during a simulated flooding crisis. Will they heed the advice of Air Marshal Tim Garden, Amanda Platell and retired police and intelligence offficer Charles Shoebridge? *9305*	**8.0 Heartbeat** Secrets And Lies (T) (S) Oh dear, there's a blackmailer on the loose. *3367* **9.0** PREVIEW **Belonging** (T) (S) Adaptation of Stevie Davies' novel, The Web Of Belonging, starring Brenda Blethyn as dedicated wife Jess whose life is turned upside down when husband Jacob (Kevin Whately) walks out on their marriage. With Rosemary Harris, Anna Massey and Peter Sallis. *6454*	**8.0** PREVIEW **Funny Already: The History Of Jewish Comedy** (T) Documentary charting the history of Jewish humour, from the vaudeville stage to globally successful sitcoms like Seinfield and Roseanne. *1909* **9.0 Who Got Marc Bolan's Millions?** (T) (R) With only £10,000 to his name when he died, where did all the cash go? His family attempts to find out. *4473*
10.0 News; (T) Weather *460367* **10.15 Traffic Cops Special: Under Pressure** (T) (S) (R) Documentary following South Yorkshire's traffic unit. *385803* **11.15 Rosh Hashana: Remembering For The Future** (T) (S) Chief Rabbi Dr Jonathon Sacks delivers his annual message for the Jewish New Year, talking to the fathers of murder victims Damilola Taylor and Daniel Pearl. *677218* **11.40** FILM **Carry On Loving** (Gerald Thomas, 1970) (T) Smutty comedy starring Sid James and the team. Weatherview *278676* **1.10 BBC News 24** *52656954*	**10.0 Little Britain** (T) (S) (R) More ladylike comedy. *84657* **10.30 Match Of The Day 2** (T) Adrian Chiles reviews the weekend's games with highlights of Tottenham Hotspur and Norwich City. *908015* **11.15 3 Non-Blondes** (T) Hidden-camera comedy show. *461763* **11.45** FILM **Dead Ringers** (David Cronenberg, 1988) (T) (S) Thriller starring Jeremy Irons. See Film Choice. *856164* **1.35** Close **2.0** BBC Learning Zone: Workskills Wise At Work: Money Matters *96023* **3.0** Webwise For Business: Using The Internet (T) *24955* **4.0** Improving Skills (T) *41110* **5.0** Workplace Skills (T) *94058*	**11.0 ITV Weekend News;** (T) (S) Weather *902541* **11.15 Not Just On Sunday** Politics (T) (S) Melvyn Bragg discusses religion within politics. *465589* **11.44 London Weather** (S) *763909* **11.45 F1: Italian Grand Prix** (S) This afternoon's race at Monza. *419314* **12.45 World Rally Championship** Great Britain (T) (S) *27619* **1.15** Motorsport UK (T) (S) *9614145* **1.40** Building The Dream (T) (S) (R) *3380232* **2.05** Trisha (T) (S) (R) *8389348* **3.0** Today With Des And Mel (S) *5376690* **3.45** World Sport (T) (S) (R) *30139* **4.15** ITV Nightscreen *3254313* **5.30** News *84394*	**10.0** FILM **Alien Resurrection** (Jean-Pierre Jeunet, 1997) (T) Sigourney Weaver's back as a human/alien clone for the fourth outing. The aliens can swim now too. With Winona Ryder, Dominique Pinon. See Film Choice. *1270* **12.0** FILM **The Fan** (Tony Scott, 1996) (T) Thriller starring Robert De Niro as a stalker obsessed with baseball star Wesley Snipes. With Ellen Barkin, John Leguizamo. See Film Choice. *99815481* **2.05** Behind The Crime (T) (R) *8295955* **3.05** The 9/11 Conspriacies (T) (R) *4517145* **4.05** Avenging Terror (T) (R) *3944042* **5.05** Countdown (T) (R) *3723329* **5.50** Angela Anaconda (T) *9714394*

62 The Guide

ACTIVITIES

1. Look at the extract from the *Guardian* TV guide on page 84. These were the TV programmes shown on a normal Sunday.

a) Go through them carefully and list the ones that have an obvious religious theme. Some have already been circled to start you off. Note the channel and time the programme was broadcast.

b) List any programme titles that might have some religious content. (Just make a guess from the title.)

c) Sort your list into three categories: films, religious broadcasts and documentaries.

d) Compare the different channels. Who has the most and least?

e) Look at the times of the broadcasts and suggest what sort of people might be watching them at that time.

f) Which religions are featured in this schedule? Which ones have been omitted? Why do you think the television companies are choosing to feature some and not others?

2. Video *The Heaven and Earth Show*. Watch it and answer the questions below.

a) What date and time was this programme broadcast? How would that affect the type of person likely to watch it?

b) Note the style of presentation. How similar is it to a chat show?

c) Note the topics being discussed. How long did each piece last? What age group/gender would that topic interest? Was the topic a moral one or a religious one?

d) Were any parts of the programme multi-faith or multi-ethnic?

Figure D The Heaven and Earth Show *has recently been revamped. Who do you think this new look is targeted at?*

e) Go to the programme's website by visiting www.heinemann.co.uk/hotlinks, typing in the express code 2280P and clicking on this section. Is there any additional material available to support a religious person's interest?

f) Who do you think this programme is aimed at? How far do you think it succeeds in capturing that audience?

g) What are the differences between this programme and *Songs of Praise*, which is also a religious broadcast? Which do you think would be the most helpful to a Christian who feels isolated? Why?

3. Look at the schedule for today's TV programmes and compare a typical weekday with last Sunday's viewing. Were there any religious programmes on television during the week? How many were shown on Sunday?

AIM

To analyse and evaluate the content of Songs of Praise *and consider the reasons for its popularity.*

Songs of Praise

Songs of Praise is such a well-known and popular programme that it is worth a detailed study. You could use it to answer an in-depth question on the exam paper about religious broadcasts, or use it to form the in-depth study as part of your coursework.

Here are some interesting facts about the programme.

- Four *Songs of Praise* presenters have gone on to become bishops.
- The audience for *Songs of Praise* is usually between five and seven million viewers.
- The largest audience was 11.4 million at Christmas in 1988.
- The programme has visited over 1800 different churches, chapels and cathedrals.
- The largest congregation was 60,000 at the Millennium Stadium, Cardiff, on 2 January 2000.
- There have been 182 presenters on *Songs of Praise*.
- The programme is regularly broadcast in the Netherlands, Australia, Canada and South Africa.

- Over the past ten years the programme has visited twenty different countries: Australia, Austria, Barbados, Brazil, Bulgaria, France, Germany, the Holy Land, Hong Kong, Ireland, Israel, Majorca, the Netherlands, Norway, Poland, Romania, South Africa, Spain, USA and Zimbabwe.
- Over 12,500 hymns have been sung on the programme over the last 40 years.

PATH TO THE TOP

The following term is worth learning; using it in the exam may help you boost your grade.

- **worship-type programme** a programme where the viewer can join in at home. They can sing or pray to God in the same way as they would in church. For the viewer, the programme is more than entertainment

FOR RESEARCH

Songs of Praise is described as a worship-type programme. How have the producers of the programme made it easier for people at home to take part? List four types of people who would find a worship-type programme particularly helpful and explain why. Look at the *Songs of Praise* website to see what other material they offer Christians. The site can be accessed by visiting www.heinemann.co.uk/hotlinks, typing in the express code 2280P and clicking on this section.

ACTIVITY

1. Watch a video recording of *Songs of Praise* and answer the questions below.

a) What day and time was this broadcast?

b) Who presented it? (Check details of the presenter on *Songs of Praise* website at a later date.)

c) What is the format of the programme? Time the different pieces in the programme so you know how long/how many hymns were sung and how long/how many interviews there were.

d) What sort of topics did the interviews cover? What had religion got to do with them?

e) Make notes on the age group and gender of the people who appeared on the programme. Look at the age and gender of the worshippers. Can you deduce anything about who the programme is aimed at?

f) What do you think regular viewers enjoy about the programme?

g) What might put some viewers off watching *Songs of Praise*?

h) If you know a family member or friend who watches *Songs of Praise* occasionally or regularly, ask them what they like about the programme.

ACTIVITIES

2. Outline the content of *Songs of Praise* and explain why some people might find it interesting. Use the notes you made when you watched *Songs of Praise* at the beginning of this lesson as the basis for your answer.

3. If you were asked by the producer of *Songs of Praise* about plans for a programme in your area, what three interviews would you like him to include? What do you think the programme could do to appeal more to a teenage audience?

4. Compare *Songs of Praise* with a religious broadcast like *The Heaven and Earth Show* to understand why one is a worship-type programme and the other is not.

5. Watch one of the religious broadcasts that is basically a complete church service. If you cannot locate one on television, you could listen to a Sunday morning service on the radio.

a) Make a note of the differences between the full service and a religious broadcast like *Songs of Praise*.

b) Which might be the most helpful to someone considering whether to become a Christian? Why?

c) What would be the disadvantages of the full service for viewers at home?

Figure E Songs of Praise *is the most popular religious programme on television at the moment. It takes four days to record the interviews and outdoor material that will be slotted between the hymn singing. Why do you think this programme is so popular?*

5 TV Documentaries

AIM

To understand what a television documentary is and to be able to evaluate the treatment of a religious theme in the programme.

What is a television documentary?

A documentary is a factual film or programme about a serious subject. It is based on things that have happened. There may be some re-enactments of conversations that people had in the past, with actors playing those parts, but they are scenes and conversations that are known to have taken place. Many of the schools broadcasts that you might watch in RE are short documentaries.

The aim of a documentary is to inform the viewer about an issue. You need to assess how well the documentary informs the viewer and, in particular, whether the information given is fair to all concerned, or whether it is biased.

For your GCSE RE exam you need to study a documentary that has a religious theme. This will provide you with material to answer questions in the section on religious broadcasts.

Everyman

Everyman is a BBC documentary series which covers interesting aspects of religion and beliefs. It is an occasional series and is often supported by a fact sheet which can be downloaded from the Internet. One of their programmes was called 'Mediums: Talking to the Dead', another was called 'The Exorcist', which was about the growing number of clergymen in the UK who have dedicated their lives to the ministry of deliverance.

Figure F *This is a shot from an* Everyman *documentary which dealt with the very controversial subject of exorcism. Why do you think some religious programmes are considered to be controversial?*

Who watches documentaries?

The audience for a religious documentary is perhaps larger than you might think. Research shows that many people who say they are not religious are often interested in religious issues, provided that the religion is dealt with sensitively. They like to watch programmes that investigate both sides of the argument, but leave them to make up their own minds. Viewers also say that they do not like it if it the programme assumes they are Christian just because they live in the United Kingdom. While you are watching, keep the agnostic viewer in mind and after you have seen the documentary several times weigh up how satisfied they would have been with the presentation.

HINT

The exam board asks you to study a documentary with a *religious theme*. If you are not sure what that means look again at page 77 and double-check with your teacher.

PATH TO THE TOP

Include some specialist terms that you know or have learned from the programme. It is a good way to gain higher marks.

Make sure you have identified the key arguments that the documentary sets out. Sort them into 'for' and 'against'. Try to learn a couple of arguments from each side to use in your extended writing and gain those important extra marks.

ACTIVITIES

1. Select your television documentary and video it so you can watch it two or three times. It is surprising how much more you spot on a second or third viewing, and with a difficult non-fiction subject the more detail you include the better.

2. Write down briefly what the subject of the documentary was. For instance, you might put that it was about reincarnation or women becoming nuns. No need for any more detail at this stage.

3. As you watch the programme again, begin to note down the different aspects of the subject which the programme shows. For example, if the subject is reincarnation, the programme might begin with people talking about what happened to them. This can be convincing if the people talking are intelligent and sensible. Then the programme might move on to look at the scientific evidence for this phenomenon which might lead you to think that it is all in the mind. A well-produced programme might well conclude with some new information that throws the subject wide open again. Perhaps there is new scientific evidence emerging that shows that everything is not as straightforward as it seems.

4. Look at the different aspects that you have written down and decide for yourself how fair and balanced the material was. Would a religious believer be happy with the way their religion was shown, or did it show them as eccentric and old-fashioned?

5. Who do you think the documentary was aimed at in terms of age group and gender? The timing of the programme and its place in the schedules may give you some clues.

6. How interesting do you think religious people would have found this programme? Offer some evidence to support your view. What about the non-religious viewer? Would they have found the programme sufficiently interesting to watch it through to the end? Again, give a reason to support your view.

7. How would you have handled this theme if you had been producing the programme?

8. Plan your own documentary on this subject for a younger age group. Consider if there are any parts of the material that might be unsuitable. Write down four points that you want to get across to viewers. How could you make the subject appealing to younger people?

AIM

To understand how television dramas can deal with a religious theme of importance to Christians and evaluate their treatment of that theme.

What is television drama?

A television drama has a fictional storyline. It may be a one-off television play or one episode in a series such as *Ballykissangel* or *Monarch of the Glen*. It is important not to base this coursework or exam answer on a soap opera because that is a separate area of study. Check with your teacher that your chosen programme is suitable.

For this part of the specification you are asked to make a detailed study of how a religious theme is handled in a television drama. The exam board is clear that this must be *a religious theme* (not a moral one). Look back to page 77 to remind yourself what the difference is and check with your teacher that the theme you want to study is suitable.

HINT

Do not automatically assume that comedies such as *The Vicar of Dibley* or *Father Ted* will provide you with the best material to discuss a religious issue. Often it can be hard to get a religious theme out of a comedy with a religious setting, because the producers are actually keen to widen the appeal of their programme by discussing something else. You might well find that a television play, or one of the institutional dramas such as *Holby City* or *The Bill*, will give you more material to work with.

Figure G *Dramas such as* Holby City *often deal with religious themes that you could study. In the scene shown above Kath, a devout Catholic, almost succumbs to her attraction to Father Michael after he reveals that he is having problems with his faith. Do you think that using television programmes is a good way to explore religious themes? Why?*

HINT

Do not get carried away telling the story. What the examiner is interested in is the religious theme that the programme tackled, so keep that firmly in your mind.

In an exam answer remember to name the television drama you are writing about. The examiner will not have a clue otherwise and worse than that, your answer will not be able to go above a Level 1.

For discussion

'Television dramas always make fun of religious people.' What do you think of this statement based on the programmes you have studied? Support your answer with some hard evidence.

'Religion is too important to be used in a television play.' Do you agree? What would people who disagree with you say?

ACTIVITIES

1. Make a list of television dramas you have seen or heard about that have dealt with a religious theme. Put the theme alongside each drama and explain why people might be interested in that subject.

2. Choose the television drama that you want to study, making sure that it has a strong religious theme that you can write about. Video the programme because you will need two to three viewings to get as much out of it as possible.

3. Define the religious theme that is being featured. You need to be very clear what religious theme is under discussion. Ideally, the issue needs to be the main point of the drama. If it is a subsidiary issue you might well find there is not much to write about. In this case, look for another drama!

4. Next you need to flesh out the religious theme by explaining how the characters in the drama are involved with it. Take great care not to get carried away retelling the story. Obviously you do need to tell some of the story in order for the theme to make sense, but try to avoid including characters and parts of the plot that do not affect the religious theme. One way you might start could be, 'In the television drama ... the theme of ... is dealt with'. Keep firmly in your mind that you are being asked to give a clear and coherent outline of how a religious theme is dealt with in the drama.

5. You need to think about how the issue was depicted in the drama. Why would this be of interest to Christians? Was the problem shown from different sides or did you just get one angle on it? Were there any characters in the play who were clearly in favour of the issue? What sort of reasons did they give? Were there others who were obviously on the opposing side? Could you understand their point of view? Did you think the drama was fair to both sides in this issue, or did it make one side out to be silly or bad without presenting clear evidence? As you are working through answering these questions do not forget to keep the evidence alongside. It will always be, 'Yes, because in the drama ... happens' or 'No, because in the drama ... happens.'

6. As you consider the drama you have watched, try to think what a person who belongs to that religion might think if they watched it. Would they be offended?

7. Finally, you need to consider how the religious issue could have been handled better. The best answers will always come up with some ideas, even if it was a good programme.

AIM

To analyse a film with a specifically religious theme of importance to Christians and evaluate whether the treatment of the theme was fair or not and to consider how the treatment of the theme could have been improved.

HINT

Make sure you know the full title of the film you are going to be studying. Also be clear in your mind what religious theme (or themes) of importance to Christians is being dealt with. Then when you are writing your coursework or exam answer, put the film's name down at the beginning of your answer. Make sure you state clearly what issue is being portrayed.

Choosing the film

There are many films you could watch that have religious themes; *Four Weddings and a Funeral* is only one of them. Some other popular choices, which have been released some time ago so are easy to get hold of on video or DVD, are *Sister Act*, *Contact* and *Leap of Faith*. Choosing one on video or DVD is wise because you will probably need to watch it at least twice.

Figure H *This is a marriage scene from the film* Four Weddings and a Funeral. *Do you think comedies, like this film, can successfully convey profound religious themes concerning love and the purpose of marriage? Why?*

First viewing

Just enjoy it! You need to understand what the story is about, where the religious themes are and the general impression the whole film makes on you.

- In a couple of sentences sum up the story of the film. Be strict with yourself about using two sentences only. As in an English lesson, it is vital that you develop the ability to sum up a plot.
- Read the following summary: the film *Four Weddings and a Funeral* follows the fortunes of a group of friends in different relationships. It looks at the way people fall in love and commit themselves, including a homosexual couple.

  When you have seen that film you might like to improve on this brief outline.

The second viewing

Now the serious work begins. Have a notepad ready and, if at all possible, be in a position to pause the film at crucial times while you make a few notes.

- Under your outline of the story of the film, write down what the religious theme is. (It is possible in some films, such as *Priest*, that the main story and the religious theme are much the same.)
- Look at the way the religious theme is handled. How does the film producer put over the difficulties or conflicts involved? In the case of *Four Weddings and a Funeral*, humour is used to good effect. Although some of the situations are extremely funny and the audience cannot help but laugh, there is a serious and often sad side to what is happening to the people involved. An interesting comparison can be made between the various couples getting married and the love between the homosexual couple in the film, whose relationship would be unacceptable to many Christians. The film shows the gay couple to have deeper, truer feelings for each other than the heterosexual couples. There are also several other themes raised in this film that would interest Christians, such as the purpose of life and of death, pre-marital sex and the idea of marriage and commitment.

- How fair do you think the treatment of religion is in the film you are studying? *Four Weddings and a Funeral* shows parts of four religious wedding ceremonies. You might like to consider whether these give an accurate idea of the importance of marriage to Christians, or whether the ceremonies are only used to create funny episodes. This is also a film in which you will be looking to see if Christianity is portrayed fairly. Are there any incidents in the film that you think would offend Christians or show them in an unfair light?

- When the film is finished and you look back over your notes, try to think of ways in which the treatment of the religious theme could have been improved.

- Finally, what did you think of the film?

HINT

The film you are asked to study for this part of the exam, or for your coursework, must have a *religious theme* rather than a moral one. Check with your teacher if you are unsure whether your choice is acceptable.

ACTIVITIES

1. Describe the religious theme that was presented in the film you watched.

2. Explain why this is an important theme.

3. Do you think the treatment was fair to Christians?

Figure I *This is a scene from the soap opera* Coronation Street *when Katy tells Martin that she is pregnant after coming off the pill behind his back. Their relationship is already controversial because he is so much older than her. What other religious or moral themes has this soap opera dealt with that you could write about in an answer?*

This section of the exam paper is like the coursework section and usually there are three parts to the question.

1. The **(a)** part of this question requires a description. In simple terms, the examiner is asking you to say *what* is going on.
2. The **(b)** part of the question requires an explanation, so you are being asked to tell the examiner *why* that is happening.
3. The **(c)** part of this question is the evaluative part. The exam specification, which appears on page 77, states that you will be asked to make a personal evaluation of the way religion is dealt with in the media. That is what question **9 (c)** will be about, although you do not know exactly what you will be asked. Nevertheless, you can prepare yourself well to answer this sort of question.

Trying out your answers

Working with a partner is a really good way of practising your answers to these questions and revising material for the exam. The advantage is that your partner can prompt you with little bits of the question at a time. Often that will stop you from wandering off into just telling the story. People also find it easier to talk their answer through first because it sorts out their thoughts. Writing it up afterwards seems much easier. There is also the advantage of listening to someone else tackle the question. It lets you decide what worked and what could have been improved.

To practise answering **(a)** questions, start with one of you saying: 'Describe how a film, or television drama, handled a religious theme of importance to Christians'. You can reply by giving the name of the programme you watched. Then say what religious theme it tackled. That now opens the way for you to describe how that theme was handled. This technique can also be used to practise answering **(b)** and **(c)** questions. One of you asks the other 'Why is that an important theme?' After the answer has been given, the partner asks 'Do you think they treated the theme fairly?' When you have finished you will find that most of what you have said to your partner can be put down on paper and you have worked out a good answer.

Tackling an exam question

Here is a **(c)** question from the exam paper.

> *'The media usually makes religious people out to be old-fashioned and out-of-touch.'*
>
> Do you agree? Give reasons for your answer showing you have considered another point of view. In your answer you should refer to Christianity. **(8)**

Student's answer

Level 1 (2 marks)
For a point of view supported by one relevant reason.

Level 2 (4 marks)
For a basic for and against, or a reasoned opinion, or well argued points of view with no personal opinion.

Level 3 (6 marks)
For a reasoned personal opinion, using religious/moral argument, referring to another point of view.

Level 4 (8 marks)
For a coherent, reasoned personal opinion using religious/moral argument, evaluating another point of view to reach a personal conclusion.

I do not agree with this statement because some television programmes do show the good work religious charities do. I saw a programme on BBC 1 about the work of Christian Aid and it showed how Christians had persuaded people in Africa to give their guns up in exchange for food. ✓ (L1) The project worked really well because it made the area safer for the inhabitants by getting guns off the streets and at the same time it helped to feed the hungry. The Christians involved in that project were shown to be caring people and very aware of what was going on. I wouldn't have said there was anything old-fashioned or out-of-touch about what they were doing. Far from it. ✓ (L2)

On the other hand, I have seen some programmes where they show a church that is full of old people. That leaves you with the idea that Christians are all past it. That is not fair really because not all church-goers are old and doddery. It is a bit of a stereotype. I think the press, which is another form of the media, is more likely to treat religious people unfairly. ✓ (L3) The tabloids do not often cover religious topics unless there are some celebs involved, they are quite keen on commenting on Madonna and her different religious experiments for example. Because it is Madonna I wouldn't say they make her out to be old-fashioned, but they do tend to report it as though she is a bit out-of-touch.

Overall, I would say that television documentaries do not make religious people out to be old-fashioned and out-of-touch, but the tabloid press does sometimes. ✓ (L4)

Examiner's comments

The student's answer is a good one because she has considered both sides of the argument and given good examples relating to religion. It is a coherent and well-balanced argument followed by a personal conclusion. The final reference to the tabloid press was unexpected but clever. This answer would give the Student Level 4, 8 marks.

RELIGION AND THE MEDIA

9 a) Choose your programme carefully. It must not be a soap opera or you will lose all your marks. Keep your focus on how the theme was handled. Remember, it has to be a religious theme. Do not tell the story in detail; there are no marks for that.

b) There are two parts to this. Firstly, state why is it an important religious theme and, secondly, comment on the fairness of the portrayal.

c) This is your chance to give a personal opinion. Say *what* you think and *why*. Then say what other people think and why. Come to a conclusion. Page 123 gives tips on this type of evaluative answer.

The first (a) question and the second (b) question are both taken from Edexcel Unit B paper 2004. The first (b) question is based on a question from the Edexcel Unit B Specimen Paper.

SECTION FIVE OPTIONS: EXTENDED WRITING

You must answer ONE question from this section. You are advised to spend 30 minutes on this section. You will be assessed on the Quality of Written Communication in this section.

EXAMPLE QUESTION 9

9 a) Outline how **ONE** film or television drama (**not** a soap opera) dealt with a religious theme of importance to Christians. **(4)**

b) Explain why this theme is important and whether the treatment was fair to religious people. **(8)**

c) *'Soap operas deal with real life issues and that is a good thing.'* **OR** *'The national press deals with real life issues and that is a good thing.'*
Do you agree? Give reasons for your opinion, showing you have considered another point of view. **(8)**

(Total 20 marks)

EXAMPLE QUESTION 9

a) Describe the way a religious or moral theme of importance to Christians was dealt with in a soap opera or by the national press. **(4)**

b) Choose **ONE** specifically religious programme (religious broadcast) and explain why some people might have found it interesting. **(8)**

c) *'Religious people never get a fair deal in films or dramas.'*
Do you agree? Give reasons for your opinion, showing you have considered another point of view. **(8)**

(Total 20 marks)

Leave blank

Q9

Q9

Remember:
Although you are being given a choice of two questions on this page, there is no choice in Section Five, Question 9 on the real exam paper.

9 a) Check the theme you are going to write about fits the question. Look back to page 77 if you are in doubt. Say what the theme is first, then how it was handled.

b) Make sure you have chosen a religious broadcast. Focus on the reasons it is interesting. It is worth mentioning what sort of people would have found it interesting and why.

c) Two sides of an argument are required here. Give some examples. Conclude with your opinion and the reasons for it. See page 123 for tips on how to answer evaluative questions.

RELIGION: WEALTH AND POVERTY

Figure A *This is a scene you could find in any British town. Who's fault do you think it is that this has happened? Whose responsibility is it to do something about it?*

In this chapter you will learn:

- about Christian teachings on the possession of wealth, the uses and dangers of wealth, stewardship, almsgiving and charity, compassion and justice and the relationship between rich and poor
- about the relief of poverty and suffering in the UK by Christians, with a detailed knowledge of the work of *one* Christian person, community or organisation
- about the need for world development in response to the causes, extent and effects of poverty in the world
- about the work of Christian agencies in world development and the relief of poverty, with a detailed knowledge of *one* Christian agency and the reasons for its work
- about the relationship of religion to wealth and poverty and how to evaluate it in a general way.

ACTIVITY

1. Write down ten words or phrases Figure A brings to mind. Use some of them to write a response to the person who says, 'Britain is a prosperous society'.

AIM

To understand what world poverty means, the extent and effects of it.

STARTER

With a partner, decide what particular possessions mark somebody out as being richer than you. Would it make any difference if those possessions had been bought on credit?

Who is poor?

We can all think of people who are better off than us; some people are fabulously wealthy so that we look like paupers by comparison. At the same time, we can all think of people in the United Kingdom who are much worse off than us. Figure A on page 97 highlights some of the big divides that exist in our society today.

Some of the people we see on television, fleeing from rebel fighters, arrive in refugee camps with only what they are wearing. Their homes have been destroyed and their families killed. They seem even poorer than the homeless man shown in Figure D on page 102, who at least has a few blankets and probably a carrier bag with some possessions in it. A person entering the refugee camp with blankets and a bag of items they have salvaged would appear positively rich by comparison to those who arrive with nothing. It is all relative – it depends on your own position at the time.

The world picture

The terms used when talking about poverty are relative. Most people consider that in the West we live in **developed countries** because the majority of us have a good standard of living and life expectancy.

At the opposite end of the scale, there are countries where the standard of living is much lower and most of the population struggle to survive. Health and life expectancy in these countries are far below those of people living in developed countries. It is not uncommon for people to be malnourished or suffering from starvation. These countries are called **less economically developed countries**. This term is frequently shortened to LEDCs. These are the poor countries that used to be referred to as 'the Third World'.

In between these two extremes there are **developing countries** which are not as affluent as developed countries, but not as poor as the LEDCs. Some of these countries were previously in the Communist parts of eastern Europe. They are now working towards a more prosperous standard of living for their people. Countries such as Malaysia and Brazil also have developing economies.

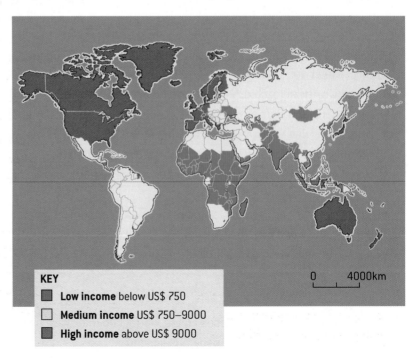

Figure B *This map shows the world divided into countries with low, medium and high domestic incomes.*

KEY

- ■ **Low income** below US$ 750
- □ **Medium income** US$ 750–9000
- ■ **High income** above US$ 9000

0   4000km

- The three richest people on the planet have more wealth than its 600 million poorest inhabitants.
- Eleven million children die every year as a direct result of poverty.
- The richest nations have a one-quarter of the world's population and four-fifths of the world's income.
- Jamaica owes the rich countries the equivalent of £1000 for every man, woman and child on the island. The average wage is £300 a year.

ACTIVITIES

1. Study the map (Figure B) and the fact box. What do you notice about the distribution of wealth and poverty in the world? Estimate the proportion of the world that is developed, developing and less developed. Remember, your total should add up to 100 per cent! Use the information given, along with what you have deduced, to write a press release that could be used by a charity campaigning against world poverty.

2. Visit CAFOD's website by going to www.heinemann.co.uk/hotlinks, typing in the express code 2280P and clicking on this section. Write down four points relating to world poverty you could add to the fact box.

Causes of world poverty

There are many factors that cause poverty and they are not the same in every country. Sometimes one problem will lead to another and things get worse and worse. Here are some of the most common reasons.

- *War:* Conflict often occurs in LEDCs as different groups try to gain power. The conflicts destroy homes and crops and kill innocent people.

Money and food that could have helped people is used to pay for weapons and armies while ordinary people are left homeless and starving.

- *Natural disasters:* Often LEDCs are in areas where floods, earthquakes, hurricanes and other natural disasters are common. These occur and recur, destroying what little economic progress the country has made and adding to the suffering of the population.
- *Debt:* In the past, wealthy nations loaned LEDCs huge sums of money at high interest rates to enable the LEDCs to develop their economies. These deals have resulted in the poorest countries paying the richest countries large amounts of interest. Many LEDCs have been left with debts and mounting interest they will never be able to pay off.
- *Cash crops:* To raise money, LEDCs have been encouraged to use most of their resources to grow crops they can sell to the West such as tobacco, baby vegetables, tea, cotton etc. They grow these instead of growing food to feed their own populations.
- *Lack of health care:* Inadequate medicines, lack of clean water and no proper health education or contraception mean many children die before they are five years old.
- *Corrupt leadership:* Some LEDCs have corrupt governments and corrupt leaders. Aid in terms of money and resources, given to the country by richer nations, is often squandered.
- *Lack of education:* In many LEDCs there is no free education, so there is little chance of poor children being able to go to school and learn how to improve things.

ACTIVITY

3. Which of the points above do you think a charity could help with? List them in order of importance and explain the advantage of tackling them in that order.

AIM

To understand the need for world development and the different types of world aid.

STARTER

As a class decide what is meant by the '**global village**'. Build up a list of things in your classroom that came from another country. Think about the clothing you are wearing, any food in your bag (e.g. bananas, chocolate), the stationery and textbooks you use and so on. Does it matter that 99 per cent of branded trainers are made in Asia, where wages range from 23p to 46p an hour?

World development

Because our lifestyle is closely linked to what happens in the rest of the world, the problem of poverty anywhere on the planet concerns us all. Look back at the map on page 98 (Figure B).

It is clear that poverty is a world issue: geographically the problem covers a large area of the globe. Equally, finding solutions to such widespread poverty will require a major input from all the wealthy nations.

Some people believe that we should help people in less economically developed countries (LEDCs) because these people are human beings like us. It is simple **justice**. Others argue that we should help people in LEDCs because we depend on them for our survival. If we want the people in these countries to continue growing crops for us, to work in the call-centres that boost our economy and to provide a market where we can sell our goods, then we need to ensure they get enough food to eat.

ACTIVITY

1. You will notice there is a contrast in the motives behind these two arguments above. Which argument do you think a religious believer would support and why?

Figure C In the summer of 2004, Hurricane Jeanne devastated the Caribbean island of Haiti. Even in normal times, Haiti is one of the poorest countries in the world – 80 per cent of the population are poverty-stricken. The United Nations has developed a food programme there because malnutrition is widespread, with 47 per cent of children under five having stunted growth. The flooding that followed in the wake of the hurricane compounded the country's problems. Nearly 2000 people were killed and the majority of the islanders were left homeless and starving. Why do you think other countries felt the need to help Haiti?

What is the solution to world poverty?

Emergency aid

This involves providing a rapid response to a crisis such as an earthquake or flood where people are likely to die within a short period of time if help does not arrive. Aid agencies have to arrive quickly with food, shelter and medical supplies in order to save people's lives. Assistance may also be needed to dig people out of fallen buildings, bury bodies to prevent disease or get power supplies and clean water supplies restored.

Long-term development

Once the immediate threat to life has been dealt with, it is important to help an LEDC become self-supporting once more. This could include giving advice and materials to help them improve agriculture so they can feed their population. Other projects might involve setting up schools, hospitals and reliable water supplies. Aid agencies think this money is well spent because it will help the country to get back on its feet and not require charity again.

Education

This is also thought to be an important part of the long-term aid for a country. Education is more than just setting up schools for children. It might include contraceptive advice for women, or advice on nutrition and general hygiene so their children are better looked after and less likely to catch diseases. People are also taught new skills to help them earn a living and become less dependent on charity.

Christian Aid says:

Christian Aid believes in strengthening people to find their own solutions to the problems they face. It strives for a new world transformed by an end to poverty and campaigns to change the rules that keep people poor.

CAFOD says:

We believe that all human beings have a right to dignity and respect and that the world's resources are a gift to be shared by all men and women, whatever their race, nationality or religion … We do not just give money to poor communities and walk away, or just support projects in emergencies. We work hand-in-hand with local people to help them to respond to their own real needs. Come rain or shine, we stick with it. Projects like landmine awareness training, farming skills training and water programmes can take years to complete.

ACTIVITIES

2. Look on CAFOD's website by visiting www.heinemann.co.uk/hotlinks, typing in the express code 2280P and clicking on this section. Find one up-to-date example of the emergency aid and one example of long-term aid CAFOD are supplying. Why are both forms of aid important?

3. Look at Christian Aid's website by visiting www.heinemann.co.uk/hotlinks, typing in the express code 2280P and clicking on this section, or check whether your library has a copy of *Christian Aid News*. Find out what emergency aid the charity is giving at present and what long-term projects it is working on.

4. 'Long term development is more important than emergency aid.' Do you agree? Why?

FOR RESEARCH

One of the causes of world poverty that is listed on page 99 is debt. Research in more detail what this problem involves and what solutions have been suggested. Find out about Jubilee 2000. What success did it have? A good place to start your research would be their website which can be accessed by visiting www.heinemann.co.uk/hotlinks, typing in the express code 2280P and clicking on this section.

6 Christian teachings about wealth and poverty

AIM

To understand Christian teachings on possession, the uses and dangers of wealth and the relationship between the rich and poor.

STARTER

Suggest three possible reasons why the person in Figure D is homeless. One thing is certain, he was not born into it. If a Christian wanted to put biblical teachings into practice, what do you think they could do to help this person?

The Bible says:

A *Rich people who see a brother or sister in need, yet close their hearts against them, cannot claim that they love God.* (1 John 3: 17)

Christians see quotation A as evidence that doing nothing is wrong.

B *Jesus said, 'You need only one thing. Go and sell all you have and give the money to the poor, and you will have riches in heaven; then come and follow me.'* (Mark 10: 21)

Quotation B has caused Christians great concern. Why?

C *My brother and sisters, what good is it for people to say that they have faith if their actions do not prove it? Can that faith save them? Suppose there are brothers or sisters who need clothes and don't have enough to eat. What good is there in your saying to them, 'God bless you! Keep warm and eat well!' – if you don't give them the necessities of life?* (James 2: 14–16)

Once again, Christians are told that doing nothing is not an option. Saying all the right things doesn't make any difference either.

D *You cannot serve both God and money.* (Matthew 6: 24)

Figure D *What should the Christian response to this situation be? Why? Which Biblical quotation supports this?*

E *Jesus said, 'Do not store up riches for yourselves here on earth, where moths and rust destroy, and robbers break in and steal. Instead, store up riches for yourselves in heaven, where moths and rust cannot destroy, and robbers cannot break in and steal. For your heart will always be where your riches are'.* (Matthew 6: 19–21)

Jesus' words above are similar to another of the quotations. Which one? How are they similar?

ACTIVITY

1. Read Bible quotations A–E. Make a note of what each says about being rich. Then decide what implications that might have for a Christian who inherited a fortune from a distant uncle.

What do Christians think about money?

From quotations A–E it might appear at first that Christians think money is a bad thing, but that is not true. Christians believe that God made the world and everything in it, so money cannot be a bad thing. In fact, they would argue that wealth is a gift from God to be used for the benefit of others. Money is not the problem, but how you use it might be. Sometimes money makes people greedy and distracts them from helping those around them. Greed may even lead some people to worship money not God. Essentially, most Christians have no problem with the idea of earning money, indeed they believe people should take responsibility for themselves. However, money should be earned in an honest way and not by exploiting others.

ACTIVITIES

2. With a partner, decide on four jobs that would be unacceptable to a Christian because they involve exploiting people?

Give it all up!

There are a small number of Christians who follow Jesus' advice to the rich young man (quotation E), which was to go and sell everything, become poor and follow Jesus.

There are a larger proportion of Christians, however, who can see no advantage in making themselves poor and dependent on others. Instead they use some of their wealth to help the less fortunate, but keep enough to provide for themselves and their families. Christians believe that God will judge them on the way they used their wealth to help the poor. For them it as a matter of justice that everyone should receive the basic necessities in life.

CASE STUDY: MOTHER TERESA

Mother Teresa, who died in 1997, was an example of a Christian who gave up all her possessions to serve God. She trained as a nun before going to India to teach. She saw so much poverty there that she left the convent, learned basic medical skills and went to live and work amongst the poor. 'I felt that God wanted something more from me,' she said. 'He wanted me to be poor and to love Him in the distressing disguise of the poorest of the poor.' Mother Teresa did such exceptional work for 40 years that she is likely to be made a saint.

FOR RESEARCH

Find out more about the work of the Missionaries of Charity which Mother Teresa set up. What centres are there in the UK?

3. Would most Christians condemn a person for being rich? What does the Bible say are the dangers of being rich?

4. What does the Bible teach is the correct use of money?

RELIGION: WEALTH AND POVERTY

6

AIM

To understand Christian teachings on compassion and justice towards the poor and the relationship between religion and poverty.

What did Jesus teach about poverty?

Jesus never condemned anyone for being poor, instead he taught his followers to show compassion towards the less fortunate. 'Love your neighbour as you love yourself' (Luke 10: 27) he said. When asked who he meant by 'neighbour', Jesus told the story of the Good Samaritan (Luke 10: 25–37) to show that everyone is a neighbour. Although Jesus had few possessions himself, he demonstrated his compassion when he fed the 5000 people who followed to hear him preach.

The Sermon on the Mount

Some of Jesus' most important teachings were given in a talk known as the Sermon on the Mount (Luke 6: 20–6). Jesus told the crowd that followed him that poor people were special to him and their suffering would be rewarded in heaven. 'Happy are you poor; the Kingdom of God is yours.' He went on to point out that the lives of the rich who had ignored the sufferings of the poor would be turned upside down. 'How terrible for you who are full now; you will go hungry.'

The parable of the sheep and the goats

One of Jesus' most important teachings about poverty was in the parable of the sheep and the goats (Matthew 25: 31–46). In this, Jesus said God would judge people on the way they treated him: 'I was hungry and you fed me, thirsty and you gave me a drink; I was a stranger and you received me in your homes, naked and you clothed me; I was sick and you took care of me, in prison and you visited me,' he told his followers. They were surprised by this answer because they had never seen Jesus in such a state but he explained, 'I tell you, whenever you did this for one of the least important of these brothers of mine, you did it for me'.

Some Christians understand this parable to mean that they must help anyone who is poor and needy because God will judge them on this.

Figure E *How do you think this photo fits in with the quotations from the Bible on these pages?*

PATH TO THE TOP

Use some appropriate terms to boost your grade. The following are worth learning.

- **compassion** understanding the suffering of people and doing something to help them.
- **justice** the principle that everyone has the right to be treated fairly. Everyone has a right to a decent standard of living because everyone is part of God's creation and people are equal members of the worldwide family of humanity. It is morally wrong to ignore people's problems and people have a duty to help poorer people. Christians talk about justice in connection with giving money to the poor because they believe it is their duty to help those in need.
- **stewardship** taking care of something that does not belong to you and using it wisely. Christians believe that all wealth belongs to God and is given to people to use wisely.

For discussion

'Justice not charity is the solution to world poverty.' First work out what this actually means, then decide, as a class, whether you agree or not.

Showing compassion

Most Christians believe they should donate money to help the poor and a few Christians give ten per cent of their income to the Church. This is called a tithe and is the amount specified in the Old Testament. Today it is more usual for Christians to put a sum of money in the collection plate that is passed round the congregation during Sunday worship. This is in accordance with St Paul's advice to the Corinthians when he wrote, 'Every Sunday each of you must put aside some money, in proportion to what he has earned' (1 Corinthians 16: 2).

Christians frequently give money to charities of their choice. Some may make regular donations, others respond to collections being made in the street or to special appeals on television. Giving money to charity is also called **almsgiving.**

Giving time

Showing Christian compassion does not necessarily mean giving money. Some people give their time to help the poor. Mother Teresa was a well-known example of a person who gave of her time. Indeed, she spent her whole life helping the poor, but she never had any money to donate. She understood only too well what was needed when she said, 'The poor do not need our sympathy and our pity. The poor need our love and compassion. They can give us much more than we can give them.' What do you think Mother Teresa meant by this quotation?

Other Christians might assist with the preparation and serving of Christmas dinners to the homeless, work voluntarily in a charity shop or sort through donations of food and clothing for a disaster appeal.

What the Methodist Church says

Jesus taught his followers that they should use money in the right way and not ignore the plight of the poor (Luke 16: 19–28). For generations Methodists have taken heed of their founder, John Wesley's advice on the use of money: 'Earn all you can; save all you can; give all you can.'

For discussion

Do you think the advice of John Wesley could help alleviate poverty? Why?

ACTIVITIES

1. Why should a Christian concern themselves with the poor? List as many specific reasons as you can.

2. 'Just because you believe in God, it doesn't mean you cannot be rich.' What would you say to that? Why? What would a Christian say?

6 Christian charities working to relieve poverty overseas

AIM

To understand the work of Christian agencies in world development and in the relief of poverty.

STARTER

As a class, brainstorm the names of charities that work overseas. How many of them are specifically Christian charities?

Christian charities

There are many specifically Christian organisations that have been set up to help the poor. Although they are run by Christians, these charities are committed to helping everyone whatever their faith because in the story of the Good Samaritan, Jesus showed that everybody should be helped.

Some well-known Christian charities that work overseas are Tearfund, CAFOD, and Christian Aid. There are, however, many less well-known ones such as ABCD (which stands for Action around Bethlehem for Children with Disabilities) and Trócaire.

Action around Bethlehem Children with Disability

Figure F This charity assists families with disabled children in the Bethlehem area. Why does its name seem so appropriate for a Christian charity working with children?

CAFOD

CAFOD (The Catholic Association For Overseas Development) explains their vision.

Drawing its inspiration from Scripture, the Church's social teaching, and the experiences and hopes of the poor – those women and girls, boys and men who are deprived, marginalised, or in any way oppressed – CAFOD looks forward to a world in which:

- *the good things of creation are cherished, developed and shared by all*
- *the rights and dignity of each person are respected, discrimination is ended and all are gathered into a single human family from which no-one is excluded*
- *the voice of the poor is heard and heeded by all, and lives are no longer dominated by greed*
- *all have access to food, shelter and clean water; to a livelihood, health and education.*

Trócaire

Trócaire is the official overseas development agency of the Catholic Church in Ireland. It was set up in 1973 to show the Irish Church's concern for the suffering of the world's poorest and most oppressed people.

Trócaire, which means 'compassion' in the Irish language, draws it inspiration from scripture and the social teaching of the Catholic Church. The agency strives to promote human development and social justice in line with Gospel values.

Tearfund

The charity Tearfund not only conducts projects overseas, but also encourages young people from the UK to volunteer, for periods of between two weeks and four months, to work with some of the world's poorest communities. Lucinda Edge spent six weeks in a Ugandan hospital. Read about her experiences on the next page.

I went to Uganda with some knowledge of poverty and justice issues. I also realised how difficult, yet vital, it is to translate what I've seen overseas into changes in my own life when I return to a more familiar culture ... My African experiences have changed my life in different ways, and I think I am entering the working world very aware of the importance of using the money I earn in a way that honours God. I also want to use my experiences to tell more people about God's heart for the poor. Buying Fairtrade goods means that many people like those I met can afford to feed their families. People in the West need to know how small things can make such a big difference. Sounds clichéd, but it's true.

The Christian Blind Mission (CBM)

The Christian Blind Mission is an independent organisation made up of Christians from various denominations. Based on Christian principles, CBM is dedicated to helping people in the developing world who are suffering from eye diseases and other disabilities, irrespective of their nationality, race, gender or religion. CBM supports over 1000 projects, helping more than ten million people both by providing medical care and by training national specialists. CBM's ultimate aim is to demonstrate the love of Christ through its actions.

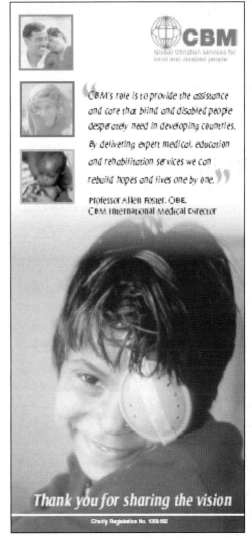

Figure G This charity takes its inspiration from the many occasions when Jesus healed blind people.

ACTIVITIES

1. Choose one Christian charity to research. It could be one of those mentioned here or another one that you are interested in. Addresses and websites for some of them appear on page 136. Find out how and when they were formed. What do they say they are committed to doing? Find out about two specific projects they are engaged in overseas and give a presentation to the class on these. Be sure to explain how this charity carries out the teachings of Jesus.

2. Which of Jesus' actions do you think CBM would draw inspiration from? You could look at Luke 7: 21.

3. Find out more about Fairtrade. You can access their website by visiting www.heinemann.co.uk/hotlinks, typing in the express code 2280P and clicking on this section. You could also look for Fairtrade goods on the supermarket shelf and read the packets. How is Fairtrade an example of Christian concern for worldwide poverty?

4. Mother Teresa said that the poor can give us much more than we can give them (see page 105). Do you think Lucinda Edge would agree with that? Why?

AIM

To understand the link between Christian teachings and the work of Christian Aid in their attempts to remove the causes of poverty.

Christian ii Aid
We believe in life before death

As part of your coursework, or for your final exam, you are required to make a detailed study of the work of one religious agency involved in working for world development and the relief of poverty. If you are studying Christianity, you could examine the work of CAFOD, Tearfund or Christian Aid. We have chosen to focus on Christian Aid. Access their website by visiting www.heinemann.co.uk/hotlinks, typing in the express code 2280P and clicking on this section. You could choose a different charity if you have access to good material or if you know a person who works closely with that charity, but make sure that it is a religious charity to qualify for this unit of work.

For discussion

Look at Figure H. With a partner discuss what sort of things Christians could do in a situation like this. Why should they get involved?

FOR RESEARCH

Choose one of the many projects Christian Aid is currently involved in and find out more details. Here are some projects you might consider:

- landmine awareness training
- working with AIDS orphans
- feeding the starving in Sudan
- providing help for small businesses in Tajikistan (one of the poorest countries in the world)
- providing education for girls in Afghanistan.

You could look on the Christian Aid website, check with the school library and with the RE department to see whether they have copies of *Christian Aid News* or write to Christian Aid (with an SAE) requesting a copy. Their address is on page 136.

Figure H *This is a scene in Darfur in Sudan where Christian Aid is working to bring relief to the thousands who have been forced from their homes by warring groups. The United Nations said the situation in Darfur was 'the worst humanitarian crisis in the world'.*

For discussion

An organisation's logo and strap line can be very revealing. Look at Christian Aid's logo on page 108. What do you think the charity is trying to show by the red symbol in the centre? Their strap line is thought-provoking because it is the opposite of what you would have expected a Christian to say. You have only to look back to Chapter 2, pages 26–7, and the work that you did there to understand that. What is Christian Aid trying to say about its work?

CASE STUDY: CHRISTIAN AID IN THE SUDAN

Fighting in the Darfur region of the Sudan has killed thousands of innocent people and forced more than a million from their homes. Those who have escaped have ended up in makeshift camps and are still vulnerable to attacks. Christian Aid reported, 'These people are in dire need and supplies of water are desperately short. The rainy season has started, the risk of malaria has increased and many families are without food, shelter, mosquito nets or proper sanitation. If the already short supplies of clean drinking water become contaminated, many people – especially children – will die.'

Christian Aid is responding by supporting the work of church groups and other charities in Sudan. They are providing shelter, water, sanitation and basic sleeping and kitchen materials for 500,000 homeless people. It is also providing extra food for 50,000 children under five and education for school-aged children.

(*Christian Aid News*, summer 2004, p.4)

ACTIVITY

1. Use the material in the case study, along with any more information you can get from Christian Aid's website, its newsletter or newspaper reports on the Internet, to make a leaflet about Christian Aid's work in Darfur. Make sure you explain to Christians why they should be concerned.

The in-depth study

- Find out when the organisation was founded and what happened that started things off. In the case of Christian Aid you will be looking at the aftermath of the Second World War and a need Christians felt they should respond to.
- Christian Aid regards itself as a Christian organisation and that is not just because the word is in its name. Find out how the Christian Church were involved in setting it up and what role it plays today. The other even more important area to look at is what aspects of Christian teachings about wealth and poverty (look back to pages 102–5) are the charity putting into practice?
- To complete your study, evaluate the work of Christian Aid. In other words, look at what it is doing and why it is doing it, then make up your own mind about whether you think Christian Aid is successfully putting Christian teachings about wealth and poverty into practice.

ACTIVITIES

2. You might like to reduce your in-depth study of a charity to a grid for ease of reference.
- Column 1: Causes of world poverty (see p. 99)
- Column 2: What the charity is doing in this area
- Column 3: What link this has with the teachings of Christianity

3. Look at the charity you have studied in detail and note down what it is doing in terms of emergency aid, long-term aid, education and campaigning for a change in attitudes towards world poverty.

4. Look at the countries your charity is targeting and compare them with the map on page 98. What parts of the world are missing out and what parts are getting most of the charity's attention?

RELIGION: WEALTH AND POVERTY

AIM

To understand what Christians are doing in the UK to relieve poverty and suffering.

STARTER

Have a class discussion on the proverb, 'Charity begins at home'. What does this mean? What would be the advantages of this approach to poverty? Where would it fail? Do you think this is an acceptable Christian response to the problem of poverty?

Church Housing Trust

This charity is dedicated to the rehabilitation and resettlement of homeless people of all ages and backgrounds. Not only do they provide hostels, day centres, winter shelters, women's refuges and drug/alcohol rehabilitation centres, the Trust also tries to prevent homelessness happening in the first place.

SPACES

SPACES is the Single Person's Accommodation Centre for the ex-Services and is a hostel with 13 places for people leaving the Armed Forces who have nowhere to go. Since it opened in 2002, 1000 people have been assisted in finding somewhere to live and given guidance with finding training and employment. They can stay for up to six months while they look for a proper home and job.

Prison Visitors' Centre at Strangeways Prison, Manchester

This might seem an odd way of helping the homeless, but the Trust says:

Over the years we have seen how upset some children can be by visiting prison and the strain this puts on families who already struggle to visit. We believe that by helping relatives visit it keeps families together and leads to less family breakdown and homelessness.

Giving homeless people a chance to turn their lives around

"I was hungry and you gave me food, I was thirsty and you gave me drink, I was a stranger and you welcomed me... as you did it to one of the least of these my brethren, you did it to me"

Mathew 25: 35-40

Figure I What sort of situation do you think has occurred that led to the homelessness of the people in each of the fair photos above?

The Centre works with the families of men leaving prison, so they avoid homelessness and as a result are less likely to re-offend … originally, families, friends and young mothers with babies queued up in all weathers to visit a prison, but when the Centre opened it offered a warm, friendly environment, with a tea bar, crèche facilities, advice on benefits and health and someone to talk to who wasn't being judgmental.

The centre also worked with prisoners' children to produce a comic that would explain in clear and simple terms what happens during a visit, some of the rules which must be obeyed as well as lots of jokes to keep them amused. The comic has been translated into eight languages and is given to all children visiting for the first time.

ACTIVITIES

1. Read what Jesus told his followers on page 104. Which parts are the Church Housing Trust putting into practice?

2. What do you think of their work in prisons? Is it sensible or should they concentrate on people like those on pages 97 or 102? Why?

FOR RESEARCH

Look at the Church Housing Trust website to discover more about their work. To access the website visit www.heinemann.co.uk/hotlinks, type in the express code 2280P and click on this section.

Methodist Homes for the Aged (MHA)

In the middle of the twentieth century, a Methodist minister became concerned about the plight of elderly people who could no longer work and had so little money that they were faced with ending their days in the workhouse. He was inspired to set up a home to care for them. His original project has developed a great deal over the years and today includes sheltered housing for older people and support for people living in their own homes as well as nursing care and residential accommodation.

ACTIVITY

3. How do Methodists show compassion towards the poor and the elderly?

Figure J *Methodist Homes for the Aged (MHA) offer their services to all needy older people, regardless of their religion. 'Our care has its roots in Christian values and seeks to provide care for the whole person – meeting physical, emotional and spiritual needs'.*

6 The work of a Christian organisation in the relief of poverty

AIM

To understand in detail the work of a Christian organisation in the relief of poverty and suffering in the UK.

The Salvation Army

The Salvation Army works 365 days a year to relieve poverty and suffering in the UK. The reason they give for their work is that 'as people made in the image of God (Genesis 1: 27), we have a responsibility to use the resources of the earth in a way that ensures that people in this and future generations do not suffer from poverty or injustice. This is part of our stewardship of the earth and our love of others. In the modern world, Christian stewardship implies large scale and permanent changes in attitudes and behaviour towards God's creation'.

ACTIVITIES

1. What reasons does The Salvations Army give for working to relieve poverty and suffering?
2. Read the case studies on these pages. Which parts of Jesus' teachings about poverty on pages 102–5 do you think The Salvation Army are putting into practice?

PATH TO THE TOP

Use some appropriate terms to boost your grade. The following are worth learning.

- **salvationists** members of The Salvation Army are called salvationists
- **stewardship** taking care of something that does not belong to you and using it wisely. Christians believe that all wealth belongs to God and is given to people to use wisely

CASE STUDY: JULIE

We first met Julie when she came to one of our community centres with her two small children. She had finally left her husband after he had given her a particularly brutal beating in full view of the terrified youngsters. The children were sobbing and it was clear they had been devastated by the violence they had witnessed.

We gave Julie a place to stay where specially trained staff could help them to recover from their nightmare. Then, when Julie decided she couldn't go back to her husband, we helped her settle into a new home. As Julie said, 'I can never be grateful enough for The Salvation Army's kindness'.

Figure K *Julie and her two small children are now safe from harm thanks to The Salvation Army. How far do you think the work of The Salvation Army demonstrates the teachings of Jesus?*

CASE STUDY: DEBBIE

Stephen, a young Salvation Army captain, was walking through the shopping centre at 9.30 at night. He saw what seemed like a pile of old clothes in a shop doorway. But it wasn't just clothes. It was a teenage girl desperately trying to keep warm in the bitter winter cold. Other people were hurrying by, but Stephen stopped to talk to the girl. At first she did not want to talk, but eventually she started to tell him her story.

Her name was Debbie and she was just 17. She had been brought up by caring parents, but everything went wrong when she got into bad company and started taking cocaine. When her parents tried to get her off the drugs, she ran away from home and ended up on the streets, begging or stealing for her 'fix'.

When she had started living rough, Debbie had not realised how hard it would be to survive the winter. Before long she was wondering if she would die of cold. In fact, there were moments of despair when she wished that she could.

Happily, thanks to Stephen, it never came to that. He invited Debbie back to the local Salvation Army centre, where they gave her a meal and called out a doctor. After a couple of days in hospital, they found her a place in one of their social centres where she could be warm and safe until they could start her detoxification programme to free her from drugs for good.

The Salvation Army says:

We give our love freely and without reservation, even to people like Debbie whom other people shun. At the same time we offer real, practical solutions to their problems. We run day centres and lunch clubs for frail and elderly people who have no one else to look after them. We run playgroups, nurseries and after-school clubs for children from disadvantaged backgrounds. We run youth clubs where youngsters can find something positive to do instead of getting into trouble. We offer food and shelter to around 20,000 homeless people every night. Often our help can change someone's whole life. Look at Debbie, for example. Heaven knows what would have happened if our officer had not rescued her. But now things are very different. She is free of her addiction, thanks to the care we gave her over several months. She's living in her own bed-sit and has a job in the local supermarket. She has even started to see her parents again. As she told us, 'I could have died on the streets, but you gave me a second chance'.

❓ For discussion

What similarities can you see between Debbie's story and the story of the Good Samaritan (Luke 10: 30–7)?

PATH TO THE TOP

The Salvation Army website has an excellent 'Schools Information Service' where you can download fact sheets about different aspects of their work for your special study. Visit the website by visiting www.heinemann.co.uk/hotlinks, typing in the express code 2280P and clicking on this section.

Figure L *Members of the The Salvation Army do more than give money. What could they do for this beggar to change his life?*

6 Putting it all together

Figure M *Poverty often has more than one cause. What might have caused the poverty shown in this photograph?*

This section of the exam paper is like the coursework section and usually there are three parts to the question.

- The **(a)** part of this question requires a description. In simple terms, the examiner is asking you to say *what* is going on.

- The **(b)** part of the question requires an explanation, so you are being asked to tell the examiner *why* that is happening.

- The **(c)** part of this question is the evaluative part. The exam specification, which appears on page 97, states that you will be asked to make a personal evaluation of the way religion deals with the issue of wealth and poverty. That is what question **10(c)** will be about, although you do not know exactly what will be asked. Nevertheless, you can prepare yourself well to answer this sort of question.

Trying out your answers

Working with a partner is a really good way of practising your answers to these questions. You could start with one of you saying, 'Tell me about the work of one Christian agency in tackling poverty.' Then reply by giving the name of the agency and say what sort of things it is doing to help the poor. It would be good if you could name some of the places in the world where the agency is working.

Tackling an exam question

Here is a **(c)** question from the exam paper.

> *'You cannot be truly religious and rich.'*
> Do you agree? Give reasons for your answer showing you have considered another point of view. In your answer you should refer to Christianity. **(8)**
> *(Edexcel Unit B, Specimen Paper)*

Student's answer

I think that you can be religious and rich provided that you spend some of your money helping the poor. ✓ (Level 1) Being rich is not necessarily a bad thing and it may not be your fault that you are rich. You could have been left a lot of money by a rich uncle or you might have won the jackpot on the lottery. I do not think God would send you to hell for that, after all neither of those things are your fault.

What is bad about being rich is being greedy and keeping all the money for yourself when there are people starving all round the world. ✓ (Level 2) It is also bad if money rules your life so that you are always wondering what else you can buy and sell to make more money.

Examiner's comments

The student starts off by making some good points, but he has not read the question carefully. He does mention God, but not the teachings of Christianity. He has not tackled the issue of whether a rich person can be truly religious either. He has just reached a Level 2. To improve his grade, he could explain what Christianity teaches about wealth, then draw his thoughts together in a conclusion.

Student's improved answer

I think that you can be religious and rich provided that you spend some of your money helping the poor. ✓ (L1) Being rich is not necessarily a bad thing and it may not be your fault that you are rich. You could have been left a lot of money by a rich uncle or you might have won the jackpot on the lottery. I do not think God would send you to hell for that, after all neither of those things are your fault. What is bad about being rich is being greedy and keeping all the money to yourself when there are people starving all round the world. ✓ (L2)

Some Christians would agree with the statement because they believe Jesus told his followers to give up all their wealth and follow him. ✓ (L3) That would mean you couldn't be rich and truly a Christian. However not all Christians agree with that because then it would mean that nobody has got anything to give to anybody else. They say that so long as you give generously to the poor, you can enjoy your wealth. Some Christians give a tithe from their income which is quite a lot of money.

In conclusion I think most Christians would say you can be truly religious and rich, so long as you are compassionate. This means following the teachings of Jesus by using some of your money to actually help others rather than just feeling sorry for them. ✓ (L4)

Level 1 (2 marks)

For a point of view supported by one relevant reason.

Level 2 (4 marks)

For a basic for and against, or a reasoned opinion, or well argued points of view with no personal opinion.

Level 3 (6 marks)

For a reasoned personal opinion, using religious/moral argument, referring to another point of view.

Level 4 (8 marks)

For a coherent, reasoned personal opinion using religious/moral argument, evaluating another point of view to reach a personal conclusion.

10 a) Be concise, but include as many points as you can. Page 99 will help you.

b) Take care to answer within the context of the UK. Pages 102–5 will help you.

c) This is your chance to give a personal opinion. Say *what* you think then explain *why*. Then say what other people think and explain why they say that. To gain the highest marks you must come to a personal conclusion, showing you have considered another viewpoint. Pages 102–5 will help you and page 123 assists with this sort of argumentative answer.

The first (a) and (b) questions are taken from Edexcel Unit B paper 2004. The second (a) question is based on a question from the Edexcel Unit B Specimen Paper.

SECTION FIVE OPTIONS: EXTENDED WRITING

You must answer ONE question from this section. You are advised to spend 30 minutes on this section. You will be assessed on the Quality of Written Communication in this section

EXAMPLE QUESTION 10

10 a) Outline the causes of world poverty. **(4)**

b) Explain why Christians should try to relieve poverty and suffering in the United Kingdom. **(8)**

c) *'Christians should give all their wealth to the poor.'*
Do you agree? Give reasons for your opinion, showing you have considered another point of view. **(8)**

(Total 20 marks)

EXAMPLE QUESTION 10

a) Describe the work of one Christian agency which helps to relieve poverty. **(4)**

b) Explain why the agency undertakes this kind of work. **(8)**

c) *'You must give a large part of your money away if you want to be religious.'*
Do you agree? Give reasons for your opinion, showing you have considered another point of view. In your answer you should refer to Christianity. **(8)**

(Total 20 marks)

Leave blank

Q10

Q10

Remember: Although you are being given a choice of two questions on this page, there is no choice in Section Five, Question 10 on the real exam paper.

10 a) This can be based in the UK or have a worldwide scope. Name the agency at the start of your answer. Pages 108–13 are helpful.

b) The answer is looking for Christian teachings (See pages 102–5). Relate them to the work of the agency to get the highest grades.

c) Your views are requested so you could begin 'I think… because…'. Then give the other side's views: 'Other people think… because…'. Make sure you come to a personal conclusion, showing that you have considered another viewpoint. See page 123 for help with these questions.

COURSEWORK GUIDANCE

Coursework is an extremely important part of your Religious Studies GCSE. It carries 20 marks of its own, which is the same as one of the other complete units of study on the paper. In addition, 3 marks are awarded for **QWC** which means the **Q**uality of your **W**ritten **C**ommunication – in other words the standard of your English. Added together this now makes that part of your work worth more than any other section of the paper.

What have you got to do?

You are asked to write about 1500 words. That sounds a lot when you first see it written down! Once you start writing, however, you might find it is not enough, but do not be tempted to go over that limit. Equally, do not assume you can get away with writing less! As a rule of thumb try to keep within 10 per cent of the number of words requested. So keep between 1350 and 1650 words.

Starting out – look at the question

This is a Religious Studies exam and the exam board wants you to consider the issue from a religious angle first and foremost. So if you are doing religion and the media coursework, remember to keep in mind that the examiner does not want a media studies answer. The examiner wants to know how Christianity is portrayed in the media, not who starred in a film or the whole plot.

Equally, when you are looking at wealth and poverty, do not get bogged down describing the problems of the poor or offer a geography answer. The examiner is asking you what Christians are doing about the problems.

Begin by analysing the title of the programme/film or the name of the religious organisation. Simply underline or highlight the important words and phrases in it, just as you have learned to do with exam questions.

Part (a)

It is clear that part (a) is the most important because it carries 12 marks. However, part (a) is divided up into three parts, so look at the number of marks the exam board will give you for each bit. Work on part (a) first.

Part (b)

Only when (a) is finished to your satisfaction should you think about tackling part (b). That is because (b) requires a thorough knowledge of the subject before you can give your opinion. This is the evaluative part of the question which you will have been practising on your exam paper work. It is your chance to give your views with the reasons for them and for you to state what those who disagree with you would say along with their reasons.

This part of the paper, the evaluative section, carries 8 marks, which is twice what it was worth on the rest of the paper. Your evaluation of this subject is extremely important.

Question part	Assessment objective criteria	Marks
a) i	Testing assessment objective 1, selecting and deploying knowledge	4 marks
a) ii	Testing assessment objective 2, explaining and understanding religion	4 marks
a) iii	Testing assessment objective 2, explaining and understanding religion	4 marks
b)	Testing assessment objective 3, evaluating different responses to religion and moral issues	8 marks

Research

The Internet is valuable for gaining up-to-date material but use it wisely.

- Not everything that appears there is accurate or useful for your coursework. Useful websites can be accessed by visiting www.heinemann.co.uk/hotlinks and typing in the express code 2280P.
- Always make a note of the name and address of the site you have used so you can put it in your list of sources.
- Do not be tempted to lift whole chunks of material off the Internet. Read and select the best information to use and rewrite it in your own words.

Books are also a useful tool for research. Once again, do not copy large chunks. Read and put in your own words the material you want to include. Keep a note of the title, author, publisher and date of publication to put in your sources. Writing to some of the organisations whose addresses appear on page 136 is also sensible and can often give you a great deal more focused information than the Internet. Don't forget to enclose an SAE if you want a reply.

Writing it up

- When you have assembled the research for the first part of the question, plan the answer.
- Then go ahead and write it up. It can be good to include quotations. Do not use long ones. A couple of sentences at most can be excellent if you go on to say 'that shows…'
- When you read through your work afterwards, check to see if there are any technical terms you could include that might boost your marks.
- When you have finished the final section of the coursework that is the time to read it all through from beginning to end. It is surprising how much easier it is to polish it up when you have had a few days break from the text.
- Polishing up not only involves re-reading and amending the material, it also includes the QWC; those vital 3 marks that are awarded for legible handwriting, generally accurate spelling, punctuation and grammar. Check that you have written in sentences (no bullet points here or you will be throwing marks away) and that you have used paragraphs. Add a list of the material you used in your research.

These are the levels the examiner will use to mark part **(a)**.
- **Level 1 (1–3 marks)** For isolated examples of simple, relevant knowledge or understanding.
- **Level 2 (4–6 marks)** For basic knowledge or understanding of a relevant idea presented in a structured way.
- **Level 3 (7–9 marks)** For a developed description/explanation showing an understanding of the main idea(s) and deploying a limited range of specialist vocabulary.
- **Level 4 (10–12 marks)** For a coherent and comprehensive description/explanation showing a full understanding of the main idea(s) using specialist terms appropriately and with precision.

These are the levels the examiner will use to mark part **(b)**.
- **Level 1 (1–2 marks)** For an opinion supported by one relevant reason.
- **Level 2 (3–4 marks)** For a basic 'for and against', or a reasoned opinion supported by religious/moral evidence or examples, presented in a structured form.
- **Level 3 (5–6 marks)** For a structured and reasoned evaluation, using religious/moral argument, evidence or examples, referring to another point of view and deploying a limited range of specialist vocabulary.
- **Level 4 (7–8 marks)** For a coherent and reasoned evaluation, based on religious/moral argument, evidence or examples, giving an account of an alternative point of view to reach a personal conclusion using specialist terms appropriately and with precision.

Your personal exam number goes in here. Take care writing it down because the number is important to the exam board when recording your score.

Here you fill in the school's exam number.

You print your surname here and your initials go afterwards. Your signature goes in the box below. These are all additional safeguards to ensure that the exam board has awarded the marks for this exam paper to the right candidate.

These columns are for each question on the paper. When you have finished answering your paper, go back to the front and cross off the numbers of the questions you have chosen to answer. Leave the right-hand column of boxes blank because the examiner will put the marks you have scored in it.

These two boxes are left blank by you. The examiner will enter the total marks for the paper in the top box. When the examiner's marking is checked by the leader of the examining team, the team leader puts his or her total mark in the lower box. They should be the same. If for any reason the marks are very different, the paper will be marked again. That way you know that you are getting a fair, correct mark for your work.

In this box the examiner will write the total you have scored on the questions in the exam paper.

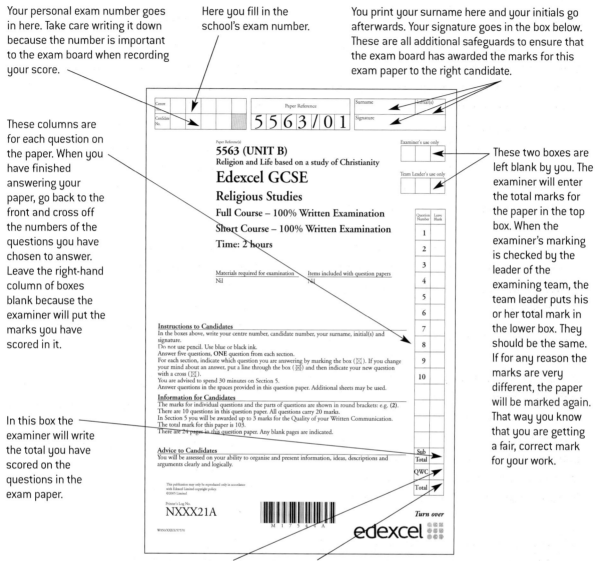

In this box the examiner will write the mark for your **QWC** (**Q**uality of **W**ritten **C**ommunication). This is the mark out of three which you have been awarded for your use of English in the extended writing question. If you did coursework, those marks will have been awarded there and will not appear on the exam paper.

In this final box the examiner will write your total mark for this paper, adding in the QWC if necessary. The total for candidates who did the extended writing question will be out of 103 and the paper will be out of 80 for candidates who did coursework. This is because the coursework is marked out of 23.

The diagram above shows the front cover of the GCSE exam paper. This paper has ten questions on it because it contains questions 9 and 10 for the extended writing tasks. If you have chosen to do coursework for your exam, then the front cover you will see will only have questions 1 to 8.

These instructions, information and advice will always appear on the front of the paper. It is worth reading it carefully now. Check you understand it. Now is a good opportunity to ask your teacher about anything you are not sure of here.

Exam focus on the (a) questions

Answering the (a) questions

The **(a)** questions are short questions to start you off on each page of the exam paper. You just have to give the meaning of a word. There are a set number of key terms in each unit of study and the exam paper can only ask you the meaning of one of those words. With careful preparation you can guarantee that you pick up those 2 marks every time.

HINT

The exam paper is only asking for a definition, that is the meaning of this important word. You only have to write one sentence so do not be tempted to go on for a paragraph. You need to write down the essence of that word or expression in your definition. Look at the definitions given in the glossary; they are good to learn and fix in your mind. Occasionally, you may also be asked to give an example to show you understand what a key word means.

Key terms

The full list of key terms for each unit appears on the opening page of the unit and in the boxes opposite. Meanings are also given during the course of each unit and all the key terms are defined in the glossary on pages 138–40.

- With a partner you could test each other on the meanings.
- On your own you can test yourself by copying down each word. Next write down what you think the meaning is. Then check it against the glossary.
- Another way of learning the key terms is to write the word on a slip of paper and the meaning on another. When you have got a little pile of key terms and their meanings, try matching the correct pairs.

The key terms for Section 1, Believing in God, are:

numinous, conversion, miracle, prayer, design argument, causation argument, agnosticism, atheism, moral evil, natural evil, omnipotent, benevolent, omniscient

The key terms for Section 2, Matters of life and death, are:

resurrection, immortality of the soul, purgatory, heaven, hell, paranormal, sanctity of life, abortion, contraception, euthanasia, assisted suicide, voluntary euthanasia, non-voluntary euthanasia

The key terms for Section 3, Marriage and the family, are:

cohabitation, marriage, faithfulness, pre-marital sex, promiscuity, adultery, annulment, re-marriage, nuclear family, extended family, re-constituted family, homosexuality

The key terms for Section 4, Social harmony, are:

equality, sexism, multi-ethnic society, prejudice, discrimination, racism, racial harmony, multi-faith society, religious pluralism, religious freedom

Please note:

The information given about (a), (b), (c) and (d) questions on pages 120–3 relates to questions in Sections 1–4 of the exam paper. The questions in Section 5, the extended writing option, have different requirements. See pages 94–6, 114–16 and 132–5 for guidance on how to answer Section 5 questions.

Exam focus on the (b) questions

Answering the (b) questions

There are two types of (b) question.

1. Some (b) questions might ask you to 'outline' something. The examiner is expecting more than one point or reason to be given. It is expected that each reason will take you up to another level. In some cases, two reasons could take you up to Level 3, but three reasons would stay at Level 2 if they were limited in structure.

   With an 'outline' question, at least two or more reasons are necessary to reach Level 3. If you just list your reasons, you will not reach more than Level 2. A list counts as a limited structure. The examiner wants you to discuss each point you have given.

   To plan your answer to an 'outline' question it might be a good idea to list three or four bullet points in the margin in rough. Arrange them in the most logical order so that one can lead on to the next. Then write a sentence about each to form an answer.

2. Other (b) questions could ask you to **describe** something. Once again the examiner is looking for a concise and organised account. As part of your planning, jot down three or four points in the margin that you want to include in your answer. Arrange them in the most logical order. See if there are any specialist terms you can use.

Example questions

Here are some examples of (b) questions from different areas of study in this book. Read them through to familiarise yourself with this type of question.

- Outline the Christian attitudes to other religions. **(6)**
- Describe the Christian attitudes towards divorce. **(6)**
- Outline an argument for the existence of God based on the appearance of design in the world. **(6)**
- Outline the reasons a person might give for being agnostic. **(6)**
- Outline the British law on abortion. **(6)**

Choose one of the questions to practise a (b) answer.

These are the levels the examiner will use to mark the (b) questions in Sections 1–4 of the exam paper.
- **Level 1 (2 marks)** For an isolated example of relevant knowledge.
- **Level 2 (4 marks)** For basic relevant knowledge presented within a limited structure.
- **Level 3 (6 marks)** For an organised outline/description, using relevant knowledge with limited use of specialist vocabulary.

Answering the (c) questions

The **(c)** questions on the exam paper carry more marks than any of the other parts on the paper. They are worth 8 marks.

The **(c)** questions often begin with the words 'Explain how…' or 'Explain why…' The examiner is trying to discover two things in these questions:

- do you know *what* a believer does or thinks?
- do you understand *why* they do or think that?

It is a *what* and *why* question. You are looking at a belief that makes people behave in a certain way. The more detail you can give in this answer the better the level you will attain. With 8 marks at stake, the examiner is looking for some detail.

Different attitudes

Some **(c)** questions ask you to write about the different attitudes that exist within Christianity about a particular issue. These can be nice questions because they fall neatly into three parts.

1. What are the different attitudes believers have about this subject? This will be a brief opening sentence or two which sums up the basic differences within Christianity.
2. Why does each group think that? This is the main point of your answer and will explain in detail what each group thinks, and the religious reasons they would give for their views.
3. Conclude with a short sentence explaining why there is variation within the religion. Often the different views hinge on the interpretation of passages in Holy books.

Key terms

Do not forget that the highest levels in this question, as in all of the questions, will go to candidates who can use specialist terms correctly. Think back to the key terms you learned when you studied that unit and see if there is an opportunity to use one of these terms in your answer to demonstrate to the examiner that you have a good understanding of the subject.

Example questions

The **(c)** questions give you a chance to show the examiner you understand the issues you have studied. Here are some examples of **(c)** questions from different areas of study in this book. Read them through to familiarise yourself with this type of question.

- Explain why there are different Christian attitudes to life after death. **(8)**
- Explain how the Christian community supports family life. **(8)**
- Explain why there are different attitudes to re-marriage in Christianity. **(8)**
- Explain why Christians hold different attitudes towards abortion. **(8)**
- Explain why there are different attitudes towards homosexuality in Christianity. **(8)**
- Explain why the existence of evil and suffering causes problems for Christians. **(8)**
- Explain why there are different views among Christians about the role of women in church. **(8)**

Choose one of these questions to practise a **(c)** answer.

These are the levels the examiner will use to mark the **(c)** questions in Sections 1–4 of the exam paper.

- **Level 1 (2 marks)** For a simple, appropriate and relevant idea.
- **Level 2 (4 marks)** For a basic explanation showing understanding of a relevant idea.
- **Level 3 (6 marks)** For a developed explanation showing understanding of the main idea(s) using some specialist vocabulary.
- **Level 4 (8 marks)** For a comprehensive explanation showing a coherent understanding of the main idea(s) and using specialist language appropriately.

Exam focus on the (d) questions

Answering the (d) questions

The **(d)** questions on the exam paper are the ones that ask you to express your opinion. You are free to agree or disagree. That will not affect your marks. What makes a difference to your marks is how well you back up your case.

The **(d)** questions are evaluative. It is the only time the examiner asks you what you actually think about an issue. You also have to show that you know about, and can state, the opposite side of the argument – what somebody who does not agree with you would say, and why they would say that. Finally, sum up by saying why you agree or disagree with the statement, showing in your conclusion that you have considered the opposite viewpoint.

Don't forget, your answer must include details of what a Christian would think.

HINTS

When you have finished your answer to one of the example questions, use the examiner's grid to see which level you have achieved. Put a tick on the spot where you think you have earned the mark each time.

Look at your bullet points. What level do you think you would have achieved? Look back at the relevant pages in this book and see if there are any further bullet points you could add to your plan to bring your answer up to a Level 4 (4 marks). Arrange your plan into at least three paragraphs then write your answer up in full.

Remember, the **(d)** question always begins with a quotation. It will give one side of an argument. The examiner wants you to show that you can understand it. You also have to show that you can see the opposite side of the argument. Do not forget that your answer must include information about how a Christian would react to the statement.

Example questions

Here are some examples of **(d)** questions from different areas of study in this book. Read them through to familiarise yourself with this type of question.

- *'God and evil cannot both exist.'* Do you agree? Give reasons for your opinion, showing you have considered another point of view. In your answer you should refer to Christianity. **(4)**
- *'If marriage vows are going to be serious, then people should not be able to break them whenever they feel like it.'* Do you agree? Give reasons for your answers showing that you have thought about another viewpoint. **(4)**
- *'Near death experiences prove there is life after death.'* Do you agree? Give reasons for your opinion, showing that you have considered another point of view. In your answer you should refer to Christianity. **(4)**
- *'Religion is the main stay of a Christian family.'* Do you agree? Give reasons for your opinion, showing that you have considered another point of view. **(4)**

Choose one of these questions to practise a **(d)** answer.

These are the levels the examiner will use to mark the **(d)** questions in Sections 1–4 of the exam paper.
- **Level 1 (1 mark)** For a point of view supported by one relevant reason.
- **Level 2 (2 marks)** For a basic for and against, or a reasoned opinion, or well argued points of view with no personal opinion.
- **Level 3 (3 marks)** For a reasoned personal opinion, using religious/moral argument, referring to another point of view.
- **Level 4 (4 marks)** For a coherent, reasoned personal opinion, using religious/moral argument, evaluating another point of view to reach a personal conclusion.

	Leave blank

SECTION ONE: BELIEVING IN GOD

You must answer ONE question from this section.

EITHER QUESTION 1

1. **a)** What does *prayer* mean? **(2)**
   b) State, with examples, what is meant by moral evil. **(6)**
   c) Explain how being brought up as a Christian could support a person's belief in God. **(8)**
   d) *'God must exist because so many people believe in him.'*
   Do you agree? Give reasons for your opinion, showing you have considered another point of view. **(4)**

(Total 20 marks)

Q1

OR QUESTION 2

2. **a)** What is meant by *natural evil*? **(2)**
   b) Describe **ONE** miracle. **(6)**
   c) Explain how the appearance of design in the world may lead to or support belief in God. **(8)**
   d) *'Giving children a religious upbringing is the best start in life they could have.'*
   Do you agree? Give reasons for your answer showing you have considered another point of view. **(4)**

(Total 20 marks)

Q2

Questions 1(b), 1(d) and 2(b) have all been taken from the Edexcel Unit B paper 2003. Question 1(c) is based on a question from the Edexcel Unit B Specimen Paper.

	Leave blank
EXTRA PRACTICE QUESTION	
a) Name **TWO** types of religious experience. **(2)**	
b) Outline the main features of a Christian upbringing. **(6)**	
c) Explain why the existence of evil and suffering may cause problems for people who believe in God. **(8)**	
d) *'Unanswered prayers prove there is no God.'* Do you agree? Give reasons for your opinion, showing you have considered another point of view. In your answer you should refer to Christianity. **(4)**	
(Total 20 marks)	

Questions (a) and (c) are taken from Edexcel Unit B paper 2003. Question (b) is based on a question from Edexcel Unit B paper 2004.

Remember:
There will only be a choice of two not three questions in Section One on the real exam paper.

Worked example for you to mark

2 b) Describe **ONE** miracle. **(6)**

A miracle is an event which seems to defy natural laws. Religious believers would say the event happened because God intervened in human life.

One example of a miracle might involve a Christian who was suffering from an illness that the doctors said was incurable. The person would probably pray to God to help them get better and if they were Roman Catholic they might go on a pilgrimage to Lourdes. Lourdes is a holy site where healing miracles have taken place. If the Christian got better from their illness they would think their prayers had been answered and a miracle had taken place.

What level do you think this answer would achieve?

● **Level 1 (2 marks)** For an isolated example of relevant knowledge.
● **Level 2 (4 marks)** For basic relevant knowledge presented within a limited structure.
● **Level 3 (6 marks)** For an organised outline/description, using relevant knowledge with limited use of specialist vocabulary.

	Leave blank

SECTION TWO: MATTERS OF LIFE AND DEATH

You must answer ONE question from this section.

EITHER QUESTION 3

3. a) What does *resurrection* mean? **(2)**
    b) Outline the British law on abortion. **(6)**
    c) Explain why Christians believe in life after death. **(8)**
    d) *'People who are suffering should be allowed to take their own life.'*
       Do you agree? Give reasons for your opinion, showing that you have considered another point of view. In your answer you should refer to Christianity. **(4)**   **Q3**

(Total 20 marks)

OR QUESTION 4

4. a) What does *immortality* mean? **(2)**
    b) Outline Christian teachings about life after death. **(6)**
    c) Explain the different Christian attitudes towards euthanasia. **(8)**
    d) *'All good people will go to heaven whatever they believe.'*
       Do you agree? Give reasons for your opinion, showing you have considered another point of view. In your answer you should refer to Christianity. **(4)**   **Q4**

(Total 20 marks)

Questions 3(a) and 3(b) are taken from the Edexcel Unit B paper 2004. Questions 3(c) and 3(d) are taken from the Edexcel Unit B Specimen Paper. Question 4(a) is based on a question from the Edexcel Unit B Specimen Paper. Question 4(d) is taken from Edexcel Unit B paper 2003.

Questions (a) and (c) are taken from the Edexcel Unit B paper 2003. Question (b) is based on a question from the Edexcel Unit B Specimen Paper.

EXTRA PRACTICE QUESTION

a) Give **TWO** examples of the paranormal. **(2)**

b) Outline the Christian teachings on euthanasia. **(6)**

c) Explain why some people do not believe in life after death. **(8)**

d) *'Life is sacred and should be preserved at all costs.'*

Do you agree? Give reasons for your opinion, showing you have considered another point of view. In your answer you should refer to Christianity. **(4)**

(Total 20 marks)

Leave blank

Remember: There will only be a choice of two not three questions in Section Two on the real exam paper.

Worked example for you to mark

c) Explain why some people do not believe in life after death. **(8)**

Some people say that life after death cannot possibly exist because there is no evidence. Nobody who has died has ever come back to tell us about it. When the body dies, everything dies. That has been shown to be the case when people have to make difficult decisions to do with switching off a life-support machine. In cases like this, the brain always dies before the body, so that means there cannot be anything left to go on for eternity.

Also people who do not believe in life after death say that death means the end of life. It does not make sense to talk about life after death; that is illogical.

What level do you think this answer would achieve?

- **Level 1 (2 marks)** For a simple, appropriate and relevant idea.
- **Level 2 (4 marks)** For a basic explanation showing understanding of a relevant idea.
- **Level 3 (6 marks)** For a developed explanation showing understanding of the main idea(s), using some specialist vocabulary.
- **Level 4 (8 marks)** For a comprehensive explanation showing a coherent understanding of the main idea(s) and using specialist language appropriately.

	Leave blank

SECTION THREE: MARRIAGE AND THE FAMILY
 	
You must answer ONE question from this section.
 	
EITHER QUESTION 5
 	
5. a) What is *adultery*? (2)
   b) Outline Christian teachings about family life. (6)
   c) Explain why there are different attitudes towards divorce and re-marriage in Christianity. (8)
   d) *'A religious wedding ceremony helps to make a marriage work.'*
   Do you agree? Give reasons for your opinion, showing you have considered another point of view. In your answer you should refer to Christianity. (4)
 	
(Total 20 marks)
	Q5

OR QUESTION 6
 	
6. a) What is *re-marriage?* (2)
   b) Describe the main features of the Christian marriage ceremony. (6)
   c) Explain why family life is important to Christians. (8)
   d) *'Marriage is the only place for sex.'*
   Do you agree? Give reasons for your opinion, showing you have considered another point of view. In your answer you should refer to Christianity. (4)
 	
(Total 20 marks)
	Q6

Question 5(b) is taken from Edexcel Unit B paper 2004. Question 5(d) is based on a question from the Edexcel Unit A paper 2003. Question 6(b) is based on a question from Edexcel Unit B paper 2004. Question 6(c) is based on a question from the Edexcel Unit B Specimen Paper.

Question (b) is based on a question from the Edexcel Unit B Specimen Paper. Question (c) is taken from the Edexcel Specimen Paper. Question (d) is taken from Edexcel Unit B paper 2004.

EXTRA PRACTICE QUESTION

a) What is a *nuclear family*? (2)

b) Outline different Christian attitudes towards divorce. (6)

c) Explain how a Christian wedding ceremony may help a marriage to succeed. (8)

d) *'Children don't need a mother and father who are married to each other.'* Do you agree? Give reasons for your opinion, showing you have considered another point of view. In your answer you should refer to Christianity. (4)

(Total 20 marks)

Leave blank

Remember: There will only be a choice of two not three questions in Section Three on the real exam paper.

Worked example for you to mark

6 d) *'Marriage is the only place for sex.'*

Do you agree? Give reasons for your opinion, showing you have considered another point of view. In your answer you should refer to Christianity. (4)

Roman Catholics would agree with this statement because the Bible teaches that all forms of sex outside of marriage are adultery which is a sin. Not all Christians would agree with that. Some would say that sex is acceptable in a loving relationship. Some liberal Christians accept pre-marital sex between a couple who are committed to each other and plan to marry. Some people believe it is better for a couple to live together in a sexual relationship before they marry than to find out they are incompatible and have to get divorced.

Christians are in agreement that adultery and promiscuity, which are also forms of sex outside marriage, are totally wrong. People can get hurt by adultery and there is nothing good about that. Christians think promiscuity is a misuse of God's gift of sex so they disagree with it. Overall, I think sex is acceptable before marriage because it is an act of love, but I do not agree with extra-marital sex because people can get hurt.

What level do you think this answer would achieve?

● **Level 1 (1 mark)** For a point of view supported by one relevant reasons.

● **Level 2 (2 marks)** For a basic for and against, or a reasoned opinion, or well argued points of view with no personal opinion.

● **Level 3 (3 marks)** For a reasoned personal opinion, using religious/moral argument, referring to another point of view.

● **Level 4 (4 marks)** For a coherent, reasoned personal opinion, using religious/moral argument, evaluating another point of view to reach a personal conclusion.

SECTION FOUR: SOCIAL HARMONY

You must answer ONE question from this section.

EITHER QUESTION 7

7. **a)** What is *religious freedom*? **(2)**

b) Outline Christian teachings on equality. **(6)**

c) Explain how the work of one modern Christian has contributed to racial harmony. **(8)**

d) *'Living in a multi-faith society is difficult for a believer.'*

Do you agree? Give reasons for your opinion, showing you have considered another point of view. In your answer you should refer to Christianity. **(4)**

(Total 20 marks)

Q7

OR QUESTION 8

8. **a)** Give **ONE** example of *sexism*. **(2)**

b) Outline the teachings of Christianity regarding the roles of men and women. **(6)**

c) Explain why prejudice and discrimination cause problems in a multi-ethnic society. **(8)**

d) *'Trying to convert people to your religion is wrong.'*

Do you agree? Give reasons for your opinion, showing you have considered another point of view. In your answer you should refer to Christianity. **(4)**

(Total 20 marks)

Q8

Leave blank

Questions 7(a) and 8(c) are taken from the Edexcel Unit B paper 2004. Question 8(d) is based on a question from the Edexcel Unit B Specimen Paper.

Question (a) is based on a question from Edexcel Unit B Specimen Paper. Question (b) is based on Edexcel Unit B paper 2004. Question (c) is taken from the Edexcel Unit B paper 2003.

		Leave blank
EXTRA PRACTICE QUESTION		
a) What is meant by *discrimination*? **(2)**		
b) Outline different Christian attitudes to other religions. **(6)**		
c) Explain how the teachings of Christianity may help to promote racial harmony. **(8)**		
d) *'Men and women are different so you can't expect to have equality.'* Do you agree? Give reasons for your opinion, showing you have considered another point of view. In your answer you should refer to Christianity. **(4)**		
(Total 20 marks)		

Remember: There will only be a choice of two not three questions in Section Four on the real exam paper.

Worked example for you to mark

8 b) Outline the teachings of Christianity regarding the roles of men and women. **(6)**

Christianity teaches that men and women were created equal in the sight of God. Some evangelical Christians teach that although men and women are equal they have different roles to fulfil in the home and in the church. They support this with the teachings of St Paul in the Bible.

More liberal Christians teach that because men and women were created equal, they should have equal roles in the church and in the home. These Christians look at Jesus' treatment of women in the Bible and remember that Jesus allowed Mary to sit at his feet and learn. They also point to the fact that Jesus appeared to women first after he was resurrected. St Paul taught that men and women are equal in the sight of Christ.

Roman Catholic Christians accept men and women as having equal roles, but teach that only men can become priests because Jesus chose men as his apostles.

What level do you think this answer would achieve?

- **Level 1 (2 marks)** For an isolated example of relevant knowledge.
- **Level 2 (4 marks)** For basic relevant knowledge presented within a limited structure.
- **Level 3 (6 marks)** For an organised outline/description, deploying relevant knowledge with limited use of specialist vocabulary.

Exam focus on religion and the media

	Leave blank

SECTION FIVE OPTIONS: EXTENDED WRITING

You must answer ONE question from this section. You are advised to spend 30 minutes on this section. You will be assessed on the Quality of Written Communication in this section.

EXAMPLE QUESTION 9

a) Outline the variety and range of specifically religious programmes on television. **(4)**

b) Choose a religious or moral theme of importance to Christians and explain how it was dealt with by a soap opera, or in the press. **(8)**

c) *'The media never treats religion fairly.'* Do you agree? Give reasons for your opinion, showing you have considered another point of view. **(8)**

Q9

(Total 20 marks)

EXAMPLE QUESTION 9

a) Describe the way a religious or moral theme of importance to Christians was handled in a soap opera or by the national press. **(4)**

b) Explain why some people might find a religious broadcast interesting. **(8)**

c) *'Religious documentaries are boring.'* Do you agree? Give reasons for your opinion, showing you have considered another point of view. **(8)**

Q9

(Total 20 marks)

The first (a) question and the first (c) question are taken from the Edexcel Unit B paper 2003.

	Leave blank
EXAMPLE QUESTION 9 a) Outline the content of one specifically religious broadcast on television. **(4)** b) Choose a religious theme, of importance to Christians, from a film or television drama (**not** a soap opera) and explain how the theme was dealt with. **(8)** c) *'Soap operas are the best way of helping people to understand religious and moral issues.'* **or** *'The national press is the best way of helping people to understand religious and moral issues.'* Do you agree? Give reasons for your opinion, showing you have considered another point of view. **(8)** **(Total 20 marks)**	 **Q9**

Question (b) is taken from Edexcel Unit B paper 2003. Question (c) is taken from Edexcel Unit B paper 2004.

Worked example for you to mark

9 a) Outline the variety and range of specifically religious programmes on television. **(4)**

There are a wide variety of religious programmes on television, but the majority are Christian. There are those which are worship-type programmes. These take the form of an act of worship which the viewers at home can take part in. To help them take part, the programme often puts the words of hymns on the screen so the viewer can sing along. Songs of Praise is a good example of this. At Christmas there are services of carols and Bible readings.

There are also magazine-type programmes that are specifically religious. In this sort of programme the presenter might interview a person about their religious beliefs or discuss an issue with a panel or show a film clip about a relevant religious subject. The Heaven and Earth Show is a popular magazine-type programme. There are also religious documentaries on television sometimes. I watched an interesting one about Christians visiting Bethlehem. People talked about their thoughts beforehand and at different times on the trip.

What level do you think this answer would achieve?

- **Level 1 (1 mark)** For an isolated example of relevant knowledge.
- **Level 2 (2 marks)** For basic relevant knowledge presented within a limited structure.
- **Level 3 (3 marks)** For an organised outline/description, using relevant knowledge with limited specialist vocabulary.
- **Level 4 (4 marks)** For a comprehensive outline/description using specialist vocabulary appropriately within a coherent structure.

	Leave blank

SECTION FIVE OPTIONS – EXTENDED WRITING
 	
You must answer ONE question from this section. You are advised to spend 30 minutes on this section. You will be assessed on the Quality of Written Communication in this section.
 	
EXAMPLE QUESTION 10
 	
  a) Outline the common causes of poverty in less developed countries. **(4)**
  b) Explain how Christians could help to remove the causes of world poverty. **(8)**
  c) *'True Christians aren't rich.'*
  Do you agree? Give reasons for your opinion, showing you have considered another point of view. **(8)**
 	
            (Total 20 marks)
	Q10

EXAMPLE QUESTION 10
 	
  a) Outline the way one Christian agency is working to relieve world poverty. **(4)**
  b) Explain how that agency's work is based on the teachings of Christianity. **(8)**
  c) *'Charity is the only way to solve world poverty.'*
  Do you agree? Give reasons for your opinion, showing you have considered another point of view. In your answer you should refer to Christianity. **(8)**
 	
            (Total 20 marks)
	Q10

Remember:
Although you are being given a choice of three questions on these pages, there is no choice in Section Five, Question 10 on the real exam paper.

The second questions (a) and (b) are based on questions from the Edexcel Unit B Specimen Paper.

	Leave blank
EXAMPLE QUESTION 10 **a)** Outline Christian teachings on wealth and poverty. **(4)** **b)** Explain why Christians should assist in removing the causes of world poverty. **(8)** **c)** *'World poverty is caused by selfishness.'* Do you agree? Give reasons for your opinion, showing you have considered another point of view. In your answer you should refer to Christianity. **(8)** **(Total 20 marks)**	**Q10**

Question (b) is based on a question from the Edexcel Unit B paper 2003. Question (c) is taken from Edexcel Unit B paper 2003.

Worked example for you to mark

b) Explain how that agency's work is based on the teachings of Christianity. **(8)**

The work of CAFOD is based on Jesus' teachings in the New Testament. Jesus taught his followers that they should show compassion to people who are suffering and help them as much as they can. CAFOD uses the money it raises to relieve suffering in less developed countries.

In the parable of the sheep and the goats, Jesus taught that if a person gives food and clothing to someone in need, it is the same as giving it to him. CAFOD acts on Jesus' teaching and donates food and clothing to people who have suffered from a disaster such as an earthquake or a flood.

Part of the Christian teachings on poverty explain that it is justice to help the poor and this leads CAFOD to campaign to raise people's awareness of world poverty and to get poor country's debts dropped.

What level do you think this answer would achieve?
- **Level 1 (2 marks)** For a simple, appropriate and relevant idea.
- **Level 2 (4 marks)** For a basic explanation showing understanding of a relevant idea.
- **Level 3 (6 marks)** For a developed explanation showing understanding of the main idea(s) using some specialist vocabulary.
- **Level 4 (8 marks)** For a comprehensive explanation showing a coherent understanding of the main idea(s) and using specialist language appropriately.

USEFUL ADDRESSES

Action Around Bethlehem Children with Disability
16A Park View Road,
London N3 2JB

CAFOD
Romero Close,
London SW9 9TY

Children's Society
Edward Rudolf House,
Margery Street,
London WC1 0JL

Christian Aid
35 Lower Marsh,
London SE1 7RL

Christian Blind Mission
Vision House,
Oakington Business Park,
Dry Drayton Road,
Oakington,
Cambridge CB4 5DQ

Church of England
London Diocesan House,
36 Causton Street,
London SW1P 4AU

Help the Hospices
Hospice House,
34–44 Britannia Street,
London WC1 9JB

Methodist Homes for the Aged
South and East Office,
Barrat House,
668 Hitchin Road,
Stopsley,
Luton LU2 7XH

NSPCC
Weston House,
42 Curtain Road,
London EC2A 3NH

OXFAM
Oxfam House,
274 Banbury Road,
Oxford OX2 7FY

Silver Ring Thing
530 Moon Clinton Road,
Moon Twp,
PA 15108

SPACES
Regional Resettlement Centre,
St Aidan's Road,
Catterick Garrison,
Catterick DL9 3AY

Tearfund
100 Church Road,
Teddington,
Middlesex TW11 8QE

The Catholic Truth Society
38/40 Eccleston Square,
London SW1V 1PD

The Salvation Army UK HQ
101 Newington Causeway,
London SE1 6BN

Trócaire
Maynooth,
Co. Kildare,
Ireland

To access the websites for these organisations please visit www.heinemann.co.uk/hotlinks, type in the express code 2280P and click on the useful addresses section. If you wish to email these organisations rather than sending a letter, their email addresses can be found on their websites.

Throughout this book, opportunities are included for pupils to engage with key skills as recommended in the specification, particularly in communication, working with others and ICT.

Communication

Pupils are given the chance to hold discussions. Discussion activities are flagged up throughout the book by the following icon: ◯. These discussions can take place in pairs, small groups or as whole class debates. For example:

- page 33 – a class debate on whether or not euthanasia should be legalised in the UK.
- page 79 – a paired discussion on how religion might be involved with propaganda.

Group discussions can be managed in different ways, for example, pupils could start off in pairs, then regroup into fours. Alternatively, pupils can work in fours or fives, then nominate a spokesperson to feed back to the whole class.

Many of the tasks require pupils to read and summarise information, record information and write in a variety of ways and make presentations. For example:

- activity 1, page 99 – pupils interpret information about poverty from a map, and then use that information to write a press release on behalf of a charity campaigning against poverty.
- activity 1, page 109 – pupils use information in case studies and on the Internet to make a leaflet about Christian Aid's work in Darfur.

Methods of recording and presenting information can also incorporate elements of the information technology key skill.

Information technology

Pupils are given opportunities to use ICT for research and presentation throughout this GCSE course.

Research activities are highlighted when they occur and are always focused. Pupils are provided with websites to use as a starting point for this. For example:

- activity 2, page 20 – pupils are required to find out more about the different religious experiences that people might have had at Lourdes. They are then asked to relate what they find out to how these experiences might affect someone's belief in God.
- for research box, page 86 – pupils are required to find out more about the worship-type programme, *Songs of Praise*, by visiting their website.

Pupils can also use ICT to present their work in a variety of ways. For example:

- activity 1, page 25 – pupils can put together a PowerPoint presentation showing the contrasting views people hold about life after death.
- activity 1, page 74 – pupils create a poster to show the different views Christians hold about the roles of men and women within the church.

Working with others

Many of the tasks encourage pupils to work collaboratively in both one-to-one and group situations to produce an outcome. For example:

- activity 3, page 31 – pupils are required to engage in a role play between a pregnant girl and her boyfriend.
- activity 3, page 79 – as a class pupils have to decide what the word propaganda means.

abortion the removal of a foetus from the womb before it can survive

adultery an act of sexual intercourse between a married person and someone other than their marriage partner

agnosticism not being sure whether God exists

almsgiving an old-fashioned word that means giving to charity

annulment a declaration by the Church that a marriage never lawfully existed

assisted suicide providing a seriously ill person with the means to commit suicide

atheism believing that God does not exist

believer a person who is convinced of the truth of a religion

benevolent the belief that God is good/kind

causation argument the idea that everything has been caused (started off) by something else

celibate a person who chooses not to marry or have sex

circumcision the surgical removal of the foreskin of the penis for religious reasons in Islam and Judaism

cohabitation living together without being married

communion of saints the bond between all Christians alive and dead living on earth or in heaven

compassion understanding the suffering of people and doing something to help them

confirmation a ceremony where a Christian chooses to renew the promises made on their behalf at baptism

contraception preventing conception from occurring

conversion when your life is changed by giving yourself to God

Creed a statement of Christian beliefs

design argument when things are connected and seem to have a purpose, e.g. the eye is designed for seeing

developed countries countries where most people have a good standard of living and a high life expectancy

developing countries countries moving towards a more prosperous standard of living

discrimination putting prejudice into practice and treating people less favourably because of their race/gender/colour/class

doctrine of double effect the idea that deciding to perform one action can trigger another. For example, a woman might receive treatment for cancer of the womb that, in the process, kills her unborn child. This would not be classed as abortion because the doctor set out to cure the cancer, not to cause an abortion

equality the state of everyone having equal rights regardless of gender/race/class

euthanasia an easy and gentle death

exclusivism only selected groups can take part

extended family children, parents and grandparents/aunts/uncles living as a unit or in close proximity

faithfulness staying with your marriage partner and having sex only with them

global village in the twenty-first century, transport and communication links are so swift that we can contact peoople anywhere on the planet as easily as we can contact people in a neighbouring village

heaven a place of paradise where God rules

hell a place of horrors where Satan rules

homosexuality sexual attraction to people of the same gender

immortality of the soul the idea that the soul lives on after the death of the body

inclusivism everyone can take part

intercession a prayer which asks God to help someone who is in need or suffering

justice the principle that everyone has the right to be treated fairly

less economically developed countries (LEDCs) poor countries where most people struggle to survive

marriage the condition of a man and woman legally united for the purpose of living together and, usually, having children

miracle something which seems to break a law of science and makes you think only God could have done it

moral evil actions done by humans which cause suffering

moral issues issues concerned with whether an action is right or wrong. Although the religions will have something to say about it, people who do not believe in any religion are also likely to have opinions about what is right and wrong. Issues such as abortion and stealing could be considered moral issues. These are also sometimes referred to as ethical issues

multi-ethnic society many different races and cultures living together in one society

multi-faith society many different religions living together in one society

mystical experience a spiritual feeling

natural evil things which cause suffering but have nothing to do with humans, e.g. earthquakes

non-voluntary euthanasia ending someone's life painlessly when they are unable to ask, but you have good reason for thinking they would want you to do so, e.g. switching off a life-support machine

nuclear family mother, father and children living as a unit

numinous the feeling of the presence of something greater than you, e.g. in a church or looking up at the stars

omnipotent the belief that God is all-powerful

omniscient the belief that God knows everything that has happened and everything that is going to happen

paranormal unexplained things which are thought to have spiritual causes, e.g. ghosts and mediums

pluralism different groups can coexist

prayer an attempt to contact God, usually through words

prejudice believing some people are inferior or superior without even knowing them

pre-marital sex sex before marriage

promiscuity having sex with a number of partners without commitment

propaganda information given out by an organisation which is designed to persuade people to think along certain lines

purgatory a place where Catholics believe souls go after death to be purified

racial harmony different races/colours living together happily

racism the belief that some races are superior to others

re-constituted family where two sets of children (step-brothers and sisters) become one family when their divorced parents marry each other

religious freedom the right to practise your religion or change your religion

religious issues issues which involve discussion about life and ultimate questions such as 'Why am I here?' or 'What happens when I die?' which religions may attempt to answer. Alternatively, more straightforward questions to do with the practices of one particular religious group such as 'Can a Christian marry a divorcee?' or 'Should priests be celibate?' are also considered to be religious issues

religious pluralism accepting all religions as having an equal right to coexist

re-marriage marrying again after being divorced from a previous marriage

resurrection the belief that, after death, the body stays in the grave until the end of the world when it is raised

salvationists members of The Salvation Army are called salvationists

sanctity of life the belief that life is holy and belongs to God

sexism discriminating against people because of their gender (being male or female)

stewardship taking care of something that does not belong to you and using it wisely. Christians believe that all wealth belongs to God and is given to us to use wisely

voluntary euthanasia the situation where someone dying in pain asks a doctor to end her/his life painlessly

worship-type programme a programme where the viewer can join in at home. They can sing or pray to God in the same way as they would in church. For the viewer, the programme is more than entertainment

INDEX

Bold indicates a glossary entry. Italic indicates an exam focus question.